# THE
# OLD GRAMMAR SCHOOLS

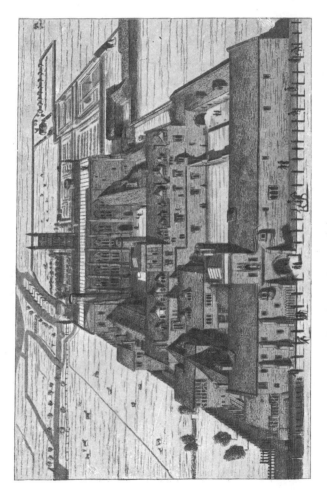

Winchester College (1393 A.D.)

# THE OLD
# GRAMMAR SCHOOLS

BY

## FOSTER WATSON

Reprints of Economic Classics

AUGUSTUS M. KELLEY PUBLISHERS

*New York 1969*

Published by
FRANK   CASS   AND   COMPANY   LIMITED
67 Great Russell Street, London WC1
by arrangement with Cambridge University Press


Published in the United States by
Augustus M. Kelley, Publishers
New York, New York 10010


First edition               1916
New impression              1968


SBN 678 05084 8


Library of Congress Catalog Card No. 75–93270

*Printed in Holland by*
*N.V. Grafische Industrie Haarlem*

# PREFACE

At the time when the English Grammar Schools were most flourishing, namely the 17th century, they subserved a practical national aim. Puritan England, by no means concerned with the teaching of the Classics *per se*, looked to the Grammar Schools for that subsidiary help which the study of Latin, Greek and Hebrew afforded to the intensive study of the Scriptures and *pietas literata*. The Grammar Schools were regarded as a great instrument in building up in our country a new theocracy, already foreshadowed by Geneva. The dominating aim of education at that time and for the next generation was, in the words of Professor Patten, 'the visualisation' of the old theocratic dispensation of the Hebrews. Undoubtedly the 'holy languages' helped the general aim; and the classical aspects of those languages 'were added unto them,' sometimes very effectively; often, it must be added, with much searching of heart.

With the collapse of the Puritan ideal as a national scheme of life, and the self-assertion of rationalism in the 18th century, the 17th century significance of the ancient languages was lost, the living force of an intensive ideal being no longer behind them. The schools lost vitality and influence. The inference seems to be that curricula are subservient to the educational aim. Hence replacing the 'Grammar' Schools by modern Secondary Schools and merely substituting the vernacular, sciences, mathematics and modern languages for the old classics, still leaves the educational question to be determined: What is the intensive background of ideal to which these subjects are to relate themselves? It is this consideration which will, in the long-run, measure the value of our new 'Secondary' Schools relatively to the old Grammar Schools—rather than the comprehensiveness of the list of subjects included in the new curricula.

F. W.

THE RED HOUSE,
   GREEN-STREET GREEN,
    ORPINGTON, KENT.
     *October*, 1916.

# CONTENTS

## ILLUSTRATIONS

Winchester (1393 A.D.) is our oldest Public (grammar) School
of the Mediaeval type.  Stratford-on-Avon Grammar School
'refounded' 1553, St Paul's 1509, Grantham Grammar School
'refounded' 1553 are representative old grammar schools and
typify the close connexion of these schools with the best national
life, as the schools to which William Shakespeare, John Milton,
and Sir Isaac Newton went, as school-boys.

'And, for a due supply of persons qualified to serve God in Church and State, let us implore His especial blessing on all schools and seminaries of religious and useful learning; particularly on....etc.'

*From the Bidding Prayer.*

Coxe's *Forms of Bidding Prayer*, p. 181.

# CHAPTER I

## THE DEVELOPMENT OF GRAMMAR SCHOOLS

Whether we consider the educational work of the Church during the Middle Ages in the Monasteries, or in connexion with the Cathedrals and the parochial system of the secular clergy, in fact, in all the schools, ecclesiastical domination is the central feature. The history of education in the Middle Ages is crucially concerned with the introduction of any lay element in the foundation and government of schools. For this reason the greatest educational name for centuries, as indicating an interest co-ordinate with the Church in education, is that of Charles the Great at the end of the 8th century. He established his Palace School, and appointed Alcuin as schoolmaster in what was the pioneer Court School. In this school subjects received their place in the curriculum because of their bearing upon social and individual culture, and were independent of the ecclesiastical colouring. It is of importance to note, therefore, that 'grammar' took a leading position in the Court School. Charles the Great, further, issued capitularies to abbots of monasteries, and to bishops of dioceses requiring them to attend rigorously to the spread of the 'study of letters,' or, in other words, to organise a system of grammar schools throughout the provinces of his Empire. It is in the expansion of the diocesan schools that we especially find the medieval development taking place in the direction of our modern educational progress, because the monasteries were essentially concerned with the training of novices, whilst the Cathedral and parochial schools attached to churches, were open to all boys, ordinarily free of cost to poor boys, and never requiring heavy fees. The actual words 'Scola grammatice' are to be found in the latter half of the 11th century A.D. ; a name which in its Latin form, as Mr Leach points out, became more common in the 13th century, when the necessity arose of distinguishing grammar schools from the 'schools' of the higher faculties in the Universities. The first actual use of the term 'Grammar School' in English appears to be in 1387 A.D. when John of Trevisa, translating from the Latin of Ralph Higden's *Polychronicon*, mentions a 'gramer scole' held at Alexandria. That grammar schools were common by the 15th century is shown from the action of William Byngham in 1439, in erecting a commodious mansion called 'God's House' in Cambridge for the training of teachers for grammar schools throughout the country. Byngham states that on the East of the way between Hampton and Coventry and on to Ripon, *seventy schools had fallen into desuetude*, because of the scarcity of Masters of Grammar. This effort of Byngham is rightly regarded as providing the first Training College building for training any type of teachers in England —though provision for a school of schoolmasters is spoken of in 1200 A.D. (see p. 69 *infra*).

But if we call all the later medieval schools teaching the subject of Latin by the name of Grammar Schools, we must note that they were of various origins, for besides the schools connected with monasteries, and cathedrals, it includes those associated with Collegiate Churches (*e.g.* Winchester College, and the School of the College Royal of our Lady of Eton), chantries, gilds and hospitals. A chantry school was one connected with a church in charge of a priest, who combined the double office of singing masses for the founder of the chantry, and teaching; and, in some cases, further duties. The first recognised case of a foundation of a school in a chantry is that of Lady Berkeley in 1348, of what was afterwards known as Wotton-under-Edge Grammar School of Lady Margaret. The first known lay founder of a Chantry Grammar School was, therefore, a woman.

Chantry Schools were sometimes Grammar Schools, sometimes Song Schools (*i.e.* substantially elementary schools), and sometimes were allotted a priest for each type of school. Mr Leach estimates the number of Chantry Schools dissolved by the Act of 1547, at about 100, of which some 14 were re-founded by Letters Patent of Edward VI. Collegiate Churches go back long before Norman times and, in their typical organisation, include the work of education. Mr Leach computes them at 200 in number in 1547. The Act of dissolution of 1547 made provision for the continuance of these schools, but only a few of them escaped confiscation of one kind or other. Southwell and Warwick Grammar Schools are examples traced back to Collegiate Church origin. Gilds had their priests who taught the children of members and eventually came to maintain grammar schools, one of the best known (though a relatively late Gild Grammar School) was that of the Gild of the Holy Cross at Stratford-on-Avon. The property of the Gild was first confiscated by Henry VIII, and then in 1552 it was bought back from Edward VI. It is supposed that Shakespeare attended as a pupil the reconstituted school, from 1571 when he reached seven years of age. Hospitals are of ancient origin but the establishment of grammar schools in connexion with them is of relatively late date. Merton College, Oxford, was connected with

Stratford-on-Avon Grammar School, refounded 1553
(*Where William Shakespeare was a pupil*)

a Hospital at Basingstoke and other Oxford and some Cambridge Colleges were similarly connected with Hospitals. The best known instance of a hospital school is post-Reformation, namely, that of Christ's Hospital, founded by Edward VI in 1553, which has always maintained its grammar school. Of the 259 schools which were dissolved by the Chantries Acts of Henry VIII and Edward VI, 140 are called Grammar Schools, and the total number of grammar schools in England before the Reformation is estimated at about 300.

Considering the much smaller population of the country such a computation makes the grammar school supply surprisingly liberal. Mr Leach estimates there was one such school for every 8300 of the population. It must be remembered, however, that Chantry grammar schools would only ordinarily consist of very few boys, for, though there are some cases cited of pre-Reformation grammar schools of over 100 pupils, they are exceptional.

Varied as these grammar schools must have been in their external organisation throughout the Middle Ages, there was, besides, considerable difference in the importance attached to the relative position of ' grammar ' in the curriculum at various periods. The curriculum of earlier education, at its fullest, consisted of the seven liberal arts, *i.e.* the trivium consisting of grammar, dialectic (or logic) and rhetoric, and the quadrivium, viz. arithmetic, music, geometry and astronomy. These seven arts were regarded as the intellectual equipment with which the theologian, the doctor and the lawyer might start out to solve by disputational processes the problems relating to professional practice. The Medieval Ages were dominated by authority—and in the period of Scholasticism regarded Aristotle as the final court of appeal. The trivium was the elementary equipment necessary for younger pupils. Even in the time of the Commonwealth a contemporary writer speaks of Eton as a 'trivial' school, meaning a school in which grammar, dialectic and rhetoric were originally taught. It is essential to realise that the earlier medieval schools, even if they claimed to be grammar schools, did so usually in recognition of the Roman usage; for in ancient Rome the scholars had studied language and literature under the name of grammar. But the later medieval schools, with both the younger and the older pupils, laid their chief stress on the logic and dialectic which prepared the skilled student for metaphysical subtlety. Even the small amount of grammar studied was surrounded by 'glosses,' and belonged more to metaphysics than to linguistics.

School-disputations of the 12th century were described by a contemporary chronicler, William Fitz-Stephen, who died about 1190. ' Three famous

schools of London flock about the Church, and there
the scholars dispute; some use demonstrations, others
topical and probable arguments. Some practise en-
thymemes, others are better at perfect syllogisms...
The boys wrangle in versifying and canvas the
principles of grammar, *e.g.* as to the rules of the
preterperfect and future tenses.'

So deeply rooted was this study of logic for the
disputational exercises that Stow, writing in 1633
said ' I myself (in my youth) have yearly seen, on
the eve of St Bartholomew, the scholars of divers
grammar schools repair to the Church yard, where
upon a bench boarded about under a tree, some one
scholar hath stepped up and there hath opposed
and answered till he were by some better scholar
overcome and put down.'

Thus it would be, on the whole, more in accordance with facts to call the medieval schools ' logic-
schools ' rather than ' grammar schools,' but the
latter name arose from historical reasons, viz. from the
curriculum of the old Roman schools, in their later
stage, when they endeavoured to assimilate the Greek
language as well as their own vernacular earlier
literature. The study of Latin in the English
medieval grammar schools was not of a literary
or prevailingly grammatical character. Roman and
Greek authors were not largely read. Instruction
was oral and traditional. The Latin learned was

decadent and 'barbarous.' It was often spoken by men who had not had living intercourse with any good Latinists, and the grammar learned was such as would be of use for disputations—a type of Latin *sui generis*.

One elementary grammar there was, that of Donatus, which held widespread sway for a thousand years and more, and it was of decided merit. The name of the author of the grammar became the general term for a grammar text-book, thus both Chaucer and Langland (in *The Vision of Piers Plowman*) speak of 'learning a donat,' *i.e.* learning grammar, and Colet in his 'lytell proheme' or preface to his *Aeditio* refers to 'certain introductions into Latin speech, called *donats*.' After the 'Donatus' was learned the later medieval text-books were futile, metaphysical, and in no sense helpful for literary purposes. The movement known as the Renascence may be briefly described as the attempt to return to a study of grammar (including in this term literary appreciation of authors) and rhetoric—(which served as a systematic analytical study of good Latin style). These subjects afforded a refuge from the medieval disputational scholasticism, which had rendered all studies an arid waste, only to be freshened in the long course of the Medieval Ages by the introduction of Arab learning and thought which from the 12th to the 14th centuries brought the only 'liberalising' studies.

For liberal studies essentially depend upon the power
to open up the mind to higher issues than those of
immediate profit to the student—and the students
in the Middle Ages of Latin with its attendant
' liberal ' Arts were largely of the narrowest utilitarian type.  Students were trained for professional
success as theologian, lawyer or physician, all in the
interests of ecclesiasticism.  Latin studies as then
pursued were consequently anti-humanistic and il-
liberal, and Greek studies had almost dropped out of
sight.  Latin and Greek ' grammar schools ' had
started from ancient Rome with the noblest ideals,
but the greatest downfall is from the greatest height,
*optimi corruptio pessima.*

## CHAPTER II

### THE GRAMMAR SCHOOLS AND THE RENASCENCE

If we judge the English medieval grammar
schools by a utilitarian standard, they were highly
successful.  They provided scholars well equipped
for the various professions.  All professional men
needed Latin ; so, too, did merchants, clerks, all
who had to make records.  Ambassadors, travellers
and secretaries naturally had to speak Latin, for

there was no other international language. Hence
Latin-speaking was essential; the Statutes of
Trinity College, Cambridge, and other colleges laid
down that Latin Grammar should not be taught
in the Colleges, except to choristers, since it was
assumed that Latin as a spoken language had been
fairly well acquired by the student before entrance.
'Boys heard Latin spoken at Church and in school
and on certain occasions they were not allowed to
talk anything else.' The relative success of the Latin
oral instruction of the pre-Reformation grammar
schools cannot be better illustrated than by the testi-
mony of that remarkable John Palsgrave who in
1530 wrote a book on French grammar, which surpassed any French grammar produced in France
itself. He further made a translation of the well-
known Latin comedy of *Acolastus* in 1540, and
advocated a series of similar translations from Latin
into English, on the ground that many schoolmasters
*knew less English than Latin.* 'They can write an
epistle right Latin-like, and thereto speak Latin as
the time shall minister occasion very well, yea, and
have also by their diligence attained to a comely vein
in making verses; yet for all this, partly because
of the rude language used in their native countries
where they were born and first learned their grammar
rules, and partly because that, coming straight from
thence unto one of your grace's universities, since

they have not had occasions to be conversant in
such places of your realm where the purest English
is spoken, *they be not able to express their conceit in
their vulgar tongue*, nor be sufficient perfectly to
open the diversities of phrases between our tongue
and the Latin (which in my poor judgment is the
very chief thing that the schoolmaster should travail
in).'

But if the Latin of the medieval schoolmasters is
allowed to have been often more fluent, or at least
more comprehensible, than their vernacular, as
Palsgrave more than suggests, yet their Latin was
of a corrupt ' barbarous ' kind.   Erasmus in the
*Praise of Folly* ridicules both the bad grammar and
the almost incredibly incorrect language thus spoken.
Vives, another humanist, a contemporary of Erasmus,
says that if Cicero came to life again, he would not
understand what was meant by the Latin commonly
used by disputants in the Universities and in the
boys' schools, whilst the scholastic dialectic was so
subtly elaborated that it became almost another
art from that of the original Aristotelian logic.

Yet Latin was used conversationally by the church-
men, statesmen, and academic scholars in England
to an extent which would compare favourably with
the Greek speaking by the ancient Romans.   The
grammar schools endeavoured to supply a sufficient
number of men ' for Church and State ' and the civil

occupations which required a working knowledge of Latin. In other words, Latin was a subject needed by the immediate environment of all officials and was provided exactly on those lines which enabled its students to attain the proficiency suited to their future pursuits, *i.e.* the medieval grammar schools gave a successful technical education.

In accomplishing this task the organisers of medieval education overlooked the fact that by their slavish imitation of Roman Grammar Schools, by devotion to grammar and the omission of literature in their own schools, they grasped the shadow and missed the substance. The old Roman schools had sought to receive and to instil a genuine appreciation of the Greek literature and of their own older vernacular literature. The medievalist however neglected the teaching of literature. Dr J. H. Lupton has sketched the probable curriculum of the School of St Anthony's Hospital, in London. It probably included the A B C book, Cato's *Disticha de Moribus*, the *Doctrinale* of Alexander Dolensis, or the editio secunda (the second part) of Aelius Donatus, both grammar books. Dean Colet in his Statutes (1518) for the School of St Paul's which he re-established and endowed (1509), marks the parting of the ways between the medieval and the Renascence schools, in which he himself must be ranked as a leader. He says, 'I would pupils were taught always in good literature both Latin and Greek, and good authors such as have the very Roman eloquence joined with wisdom, specially Christian authors...I say that filthiness and all such "abusyon" which the later blind world brought in, which more rather may be called "blotterature" than literature, I utterly abanish and exclude out of this School.'

Literature, or ' good letters ' was the educational cry of the Renascence, or the 'Revival of letters' as it is also called. For the best literature that the world had produced, there was only one possible source, the literature of the ancient Greeks and Romans. Yet Colet, in truth, was only partially over the starting-point of the Renascence, for the Christian authors referred to above were non-classical, viz. Lactantius, Prudentius, Probus, Sedulius, Juvencus. In addition, Colet would include two modern Latin writers, the author of the *Institutum Christiani hominis*, viz. his friend Erasmus, and the *Eclogues* of Baptista Mantuanus. These he definitely names, whilst the writers of the ' very Roman eloquence,'—the classical authors, are not particularised. On the other hand, Colet wished grammar to be placed on a more secure footing than it had been in the previous centuries, and for this purpose he himself compiled a Latin accidence, known as Colet's *Aeditio* in 1527. This work was the basis of the later authorised Latin Grammar of William

Lily (Colet's first headmaster of St Paul's School) which became the standard Latin Grammar, established and fixed by royal authority, to be studied in all English grammar schools. In his *Aeditio*, Colet states with remarkable clearness and emphasis the Renascence idea of grammar teaching. If his views had been followed, generations of pupils would have been saved the futilities of learning ' Lily ' by heart, and that sad procession in the school years along the path of studying rules and exceptions, only too often unrewarded by the enjoyment and appreciation of the great literary works of the Romans, much less of the Greeks. As the late Mr R. H. Quick so aptly said : ' it has been as if pupils were started off to enjoy reading works in the British Museum, and, on the road thither, never got further than the Seven Dials.' It would have been well if Colet's advice on grammar teaching had been printed on the walls of every grammar school in the sight of every master : ' Let the pupil above all busily learn and read good Latin authors, chosen poets and orators, and note wisely how they wrote and spoke, and study always to follow them ; desiring none other rules but their examples. For in the beginning men spoke not Latin because such rules were made, but contrariwise because men spoke such Latin ; upon that followed the rules, not the rules before the Latin speech.'

After Colet, Wolsey claims our attention as the
founder of a grammar school entering fully into the
new spirit of the Renascence, in which the subject-
matter of classical literature is the main concern,
and the husk and shells of formalistic disputational
skill of medieval scholasticism are abandoned. The
educational keenness of Wolsey and the magnificence
of his educational projects deserve marked recognition
in any history of English grammar schools. It was an
age in which churchman and layman vied with one
another in their munificent benefactions to learning.
In 1500, Cardinal Jiménez had laid the foundation
stone of the College of San Ildefonso at Alcalá in
Spain and established the great University which
produced the Complutensian Polyglot Bible. In
the same University was founded the College of
Three Languages for the teaching of Latin, Greek
and Hebrew. In 1517, Jerome Busleiden, a wealthy
merchant, and at the same time, an archaeologist, took
the first step in the establishment of a College of
Three Languages at Louvain in Belgium, and of this
institution the great Erasmus was the first Director.
Wolsey was not behind either Jiménez or Busleiden
in the desire to advance education, or in giving full
play to that sense of expanding individuality which
had shown itself in the Renascence leaders in Italy
with such accompanying benefits to the environments
in which they lived. In 1524, Wolsey received the

Papal Bull enabling him to convert the monastery of St Frideswide, Oxford, into the magnificent college now known as Christ Church. Wolsey decided to provide a grammar school which should be to his new college, a ' feeder ' similar to Eton College School in its relation to King's College at Cambridge, and Winchester College School to New College, Oxford. The Ipswich School was built with this end in view, but afterwards unfortunately was destroyed. As Shakespeare says of Wolsey,

> Ever witness for him
> Ipswich and Oxford! one of which fell with him,
> Unwilling to outlive the good that did it;
> The other, though unfinished, yet so famous,
> So excellent in art, and yet so rising,
> That Christendom shall ever speak his virtue.

> *(Henry VIII*, Act IV, Sc. 2.)

But though the Ipswich building was destroyed with the exception of what is still known as the College Gateway, Wolsey's ideas of a grammar school are embodied in a written Latin address to the Masters, and the proposed curriculum constitutes an important educational document (dated Sept. 1, 1528). There were to be eight classes in the School, and the work was to be distributed as follows :

Class i—to contain less forward boys, who were to be diligently exercised in the eight parts of speech, ' whose flexible accent it should be your chief concern

to form, making them respect the elements assigned
them, *with the most distinct and exact pronunciation.'*

Class ii—to practise Latin-speaking. New phrases
to be written down in note-books. Lily's *Carmen
Monitorium*, or Cato's *Precepts* to be studied with
a view of *forming the accent.*

Class iii—to read authors of a familiar style.
'Who more humorous than Aesop? Who more
useful than Terence?'

Class iv—'When you exercise the soldiership of
the fourth class, what general would you rather have
than Virgil himself, the prince of all poets? Whose
majesty of verse, it were worth while should be pro-
nounced with due intonation of voice.'

Class v—Some select epistles of Cicero.

Class vi—History—that of Sallust or of Julius
Caesar. [It is only at this stage that Wolsey in-
troduces Lily's Syntax, and verbs defective and
irregular are to be learned—*i.e.* any such verbs as
are found in 'the course of reading.']

Class vii—Horace's *Epistles* or Ovid's *Metamorphoses* or *Fasti*, with occasional efforts by the
pupils themselves at versification or epistle-writing.
Latin verse to be turned into Latin prose, and *vice
versa.* Learning by heart, for which the best time
is just before retiring to rest. Wolsey warns the
master against over-working the pupil. The boy

must be led to regard the school as *ludus literarius* [*i.e.* the school must be a place of pleasure—a literary playground].

Class viii—The higher precepts of grammar to be taught, *e.g.* the figures of Donatus, Valla's *Elegancies of the Latin Language*, etc. Wolsey describes the details to which the master himself must attend in the preparation of his lessons and class-work: ' When intending, for example, to expound at length a comedy of Terence, you may first discuss in few words the author's rank in life, his peculiar talent, and elegance of style. Next you may discuss the pleasure and utility of studying comedies. Next, unravel the plot, and discuss the metre. You may then arrange the Latin words in more simple order. Point out any remarkable elegance ; any antiquated, new-fangled or Grecian phrase ; any obscurities of expression ; any etymology ; any unusual order of construction ; the orthography ; any figure of speech, uncommon beauty of style, rhetorical ornament, or proverbial expression ; in short anything proper or improper for imitation.'

When we think of the boundless ambition which characterised Wolsey, of his importance in England as Archbishop, of his European reputation as Cardinal, and his possible election to the papal chair, it is at least suggestive that so great a prelate should found a school, and provide it with noble buildings, whilst he also carefully drew up the directions for the subjects, and methods to be used by the teachers inside its walls. But the attitude was characteristic of the Renascence. Man was to lead an universal life, and for that the highest culture was necessary, and the beginning of all culture was grammar,— grammar, of course, in Quintilian's sense, the intelligent training of boys in the reading of the good authors who had withstood the test of the ages, only to strengthen their position through the accumulated criticisms of past and present scholars.

The important position allotted in the Renascence grammar schools to Latin speaking, and the reading of the *best* Latin authors, who could appeal to pupils, is clear from the above syllabus. Wolsey, in his address to the masters of Ipswich School, may be regarded as not only making suggestions for that school but, as he himself says, ' the welfare of our country and all our fellow-subjects,' in the whole of the schools. The address, therefore, may be regarded as an early Renascence grammar school manifesto, and as such is a distinct advance on Colet's statutes for St Paul's School, with his inclusion in the curriculum of early medieval Christian poets, who were non-classical in both matter and style.

Another significant declaration of grammar school policy in the Renascence period is that of

Archbishop Cranmer, all the more important as it refers to a considerable group of schools, and a group moreover, which might serve as standard or model for other schools, as well as having its own individual distinction in the nation's school-system.

In 1540, Strype mentions that the Cathedral Church of Canterbury altered its monasterial organisation and passed into the hands of 'men of the clergy, viz. prebendaries or canons, petty canons, choristers and scholars.' When the question of election of the children or ' scholars ' arose, some of the Cathedral body wished that only gentlemen's children should be received into the Cathedral grammar school. Cranmer boldly espoused the cause of poor men's children, on the grounds that often they are endued with more ' singular gifts of nature,' and are ' commonly more apt to apply their study.' Cranmer gave as his conclusion : ' If the gentleman's son be apt to learning, let him be admitted ; if not apt, let the poor man's child, that is apt, enter his room.' Neither Wolsey nor Cranmer scrupled to approve the confiscation of monasterial and other ecclesiastical property, for the purposes of education. But the money received from the dissolved chantries, hospitals, etc., though ear-marked by an Act of Parliament, for educational purposes, was only too largely appropriated by the King and distributed at the King's caprice, away from education. Undoubtedly there was an intention, in the first instance, to devote large sums from the confiscated property to the foundation of exhibitions at the universities, to the provision of lectures, and to schools of various grades.   In 1539, Cranmer wrote a remarkable letter to Thomas Cromwell, on the subject of appropriation of funds for educational purposes in the metropolitan Church of Canterbury.   He complains that a prebendary in a Cathedral is often ' neither a learner, nor teacher, but a good viander.'   He would ' abolish the superfluous conditions of such persons.'   In the place of prebendaries, Cranmer would put 'twenty divines at £10 apiece, like as it is appointed to be at Oxford and Cambridge ; and forty students in the tongues [*i.e.* in Latin, Greek, Hebrew], and sciences, and French, to have 10 marks apiece, fòr if such a number be not there resident, to what intent should so many "readers" be there ?...And as for your sixty children in grammar [evidently Cromwell had suggested Cathedral schools of this number] their master and their usher be daily otherwise occupied in the rudiments of grammar than to be able to attend such lectures.'   So Cranmer begs for funds to have a University College, with forty students provided for, to study the *classical languages, sciences, and French*.   He urges a ' reader ' for the ' humanity ' lectures, as well as for ' divinity.'   He even named the best ' Dean ' to whom to offer the headship of the College at Canterbury, viz. Dr Crome, head of one of the Cambridge Colleges. Cranmer's sketch of the staff for the new projected College of Christ Church, Canterbury, included a Provost at £150; twelve prebendaries at £40 a year; six preachers, each £20 a year; a 'reader of humanity' in Greek, by year £30; a 'reader in divinity' in Hebrew, by year £30; a 'reader both in divinity and humanity' in Latin, by the year £40; 'a reader of civil' [law] £20; a 'reader' of physic £20; twenty students in divinity 'to be found ten at Oxford, and ten at Cambridge, every of them £10 by the year'; and, lastly—sixty scholars to be taught both grammar and logic, in Hebrew, Greek and Latin, every of them five marks by the year; a schoolmaster £20 and an usher £10 by the year.

Cranmer's scheme for the Canterbury College thus not only takes cognisance of 'divinity' subjects, but also of the Renascence 'humanity' subjects of Latin, Greek, and Hebrew, and also of the professional subjects of physic and civil law, and of what we call modern subjects, viz. '*sciences*,' or *various branches of knowledge*, and *French*. This is the first indication, as far as I know, of the inclusion of modern subjects in a College curriculum. The utilisation of the Cathedral staff for educational purposes in the organised form proposed by Cranmer, is, also, apparently a startling innovation. There is extant a document entitled King Henry VIII's *Scheme of Bishopricks*[1] with a sub-title : ' The names of the Bishopricks and Colleges newly to be erected by the King's Highness.' This contains the details named above for Canterbury, with the alteration of the Provost's salary from £150 to £100. Colleges were to be provided with ' readers of humanity in Greek, and in divinity in Hebrew, and of both divinity and humanity in Latin, with a reader in Civil [law] and in Physic,' but with no mention of sciences and French at Westminster. At other Cathedral cities, the staff equipment of the Colleges was less complete, but a reader in ' humanity ' either in Greek or in Latin or in both was projected for Winchester, Worcester, Gloucester, Peterborough, and Durham ; and a reader and studentships in divinity were to be provided in all these bishoprics.

We are, however, specially concerned with the intended re-foundations of the grammar schools under this *Scheme*. The proposals include the payment of £3. 6s. 8d. a year (*i.e.* five marks, as in Cranmer's scheme) for a maintenance grant to every ' scholar ' in the grammar schools. This may be regarded as a liberal allowance. Indeed, Mr Leach has stated that the average stipend of a schoolmaster

---

[1] This document was transcribed and published by Sir Henry Cole, London : Charles Knight and Co., 1838. Only 250 copies were issued, and apparently it is little known.

just before the time of the Reformation works out
at £6. 9s. 6d. a year.   The salary proposed by King
Henry VIII's *Scheme*, for the schoolmaster of the
Cathedral grammar school was put at £20, and £10
for the usher, or second master, and it was stipulated
that no fees for tuition were to be required by the
masters from the boys.   Grammar and logic were to
be studied in connexion with the Latin and Greek
languages, in all of the schools, whilst at Canterbury,
Rochester, Westminster, St Albans, Peterborough
and Durham, the teaching of Hebrew was added.   The
inclusion of Hebrew, among other points, raises the
question how the teachers of this subject were to be
provided if grammar schools generally took up the
subject ?   The number of ' scholars ' (each to receive the grant of £3. 6s. 8d.) was to be sixty boys in
the following Cathedral schools : Canterbury, Westminster, St Albans, Peterborough and Durham.
Forty boys were to be elected as ' scholars ' at
Worcester and Ely; thirty boys at Shrewsbury;
twenty-four at Rochester, Burton and Chester;
twenty at Dunstable, Waltham and Carlisle; and
eighteen at Durham Hospital School.   At the last
named school £4 a year was allowed to each 'scholar,'
whilst at Dunstable £2. 13s. 4d. was to be paid.
Other schools named in connexion with the *Scheme*
to be provided with a schoolmaster are : Gisburne
(with a salary of £20), Thornton (£20), Osnay and

T[h]ame (£16. 13s. 4d., with an usher at £8, 'scholars' to receive £2. 13s. 4d.), Colchester (£20), St Austin's at Bristol (£20), Bodmin, Launceston, St Germain (£20), Fountain and the Archdeaconry of Richmond (£20). Thus at least twenty-one grammar schools were projected. It may be noticed as confirmatory of the prevalence of music schools before the Reformation, that in each of the above 'bishopricks' there is associated a choristers' school with grants of £3. 6s. 8d. a year to each boy-chorister and £10 a year to the 'Master of the children,' with usually from eight to ten 'scholars' in the school.

Whatever may have been the intention, the dissolution of abbeys, colleges, hospitals and chantries did not result in great advantage to education. Even the above *Scheme* was not carried out, for Henry VIII only arranged for six new Cathedral Foundations. The Commissioners to investigate the value of the property to be confiscated were called *Commissioners for the Continuance of Schools*, a name which implies that the idea of injury to schools, however present to the minds of the authorities, was an aim which it was better explicitly to disown and contradict. Henry VIII may be credited with wishing well to the schools, for it is stated that part of the above *Scheme* is written in his own hand. In view of the large amount of 'Augmentation of the King's revenue' received from the confiscation of Church property, the *Scheme* detailed above is not surprisingly comprehensive, but it is much more extensive than was carried out. As a *Scheme*, we may describe it as the first modern suggestion for a systematic provision of secondary education. It contains, further, a forecast of the subjects which were to become the aim of masters to include in the grammar schools of the future—viz. Latin and Greek literature, and where possible, the elements of Hebrew. It would be interesting to speculate as to the author or authors of the *Scheme*. It does not seem unreasonable to suggest that the man who at Canterbury had insisted on the election of poor men's children to the grammar school, if they were ' apt,' must have had a hand in this project for the organisation of education in connexion with the Cathedral grammar schools— viz. Thomas Cranmer.

## CHAPTER III

### GRAMMAR SCHOOL FOUNDERS.    THE GREAT WARRIOR PRELATES

The Dissolution of the lesser Monasteries in 1536 and the greater Abbeys in 1539 was followed by the Chantries Acts of 1546–8. These Acts gave the statutory ' right ' to the policy of dissolving Colleges,

Free Chapels, Chantries, Hospitals, Gilds, etc., and of course the grammar schools associated with them. All these institutions and their revenues were placed in the hands of the King, on the ground that they were improperly administered, or turned to superstitious uses, and with the implication that the funds could be better applied, notably for the purposes of education. Some of the funds were so applied, *e.g.* in the endowment of the Cathedrals of the New Foundation, though, as we have seen, the larger *Scheme of Bishopricks* shows that the intention of some of the administrators went further educationally than was practically possible to carry out. The *Scheme of Bishopricks* as well as the Chantries Acts shows that ideas of re-foundation as well as devastation were present in the minds of their devisers in connexion with Cathedrals and College Churches, etc., and prepares us for the fact that the national value of the grammar schools which belonged to those institutions was never in question.

The claim is made that the King's School, Canterbury, is the oldest grammar school in England—that its continuity can be traced from the coming of Augustine, 597 A.D., or soon after, up to the present time. Indeed the historians of the school are inclined to believe that a school probably existed in Canterbury in the period of the Roman occupation[1].

---

[1] Woodruff and Cape: *History of the King's School, Canterbury.*

From the early part of the 13th century, on to the time of the dissolution near the middle of the 16th century, there are definite records of its existence, from time to time. Yet the Canterbury School is commonly said to have been founded by King Henry VIII in 1541. It is clear that this connexion of the King with that school should be named the re-foundation, not the original foundation, of the Cathedral Grammar School. Another grammar school, that of the Cathedral Church of the Blessed St Peter of York, *i.e.* St Peter's School, York, has been dated back to *c.* 700, and there is definite notice of it by Alcuin. It seems at least probable that St Peter's School existed continuously from that date till 1289, when mention definitely occurs of a change of Schoolhouse[1]. From that time onwards, with only slight gaps, there are records of the continuity of the school up to the time of the new Cathedral Foundations, when York Grammar School was placed on the same financial basis as the others.

The Collegiate Church Schools apparently existed in England before the Norman Conquest, and became frequent in the 11th, 12th and 13th centuries, until, in 1547, they reached 200 in number. Although those schools were specifically named to be

---

[1] A. F. Leach : *Early Yorkshire Schools*, I, York, Beverley Ripon. Yorkshire Archaeological Society, Record Series, Vol. xxvii, 1899.

continued, ' few have survived to our day as efficient secondary schools[1].'

Two of the chief grammar schools at that time, and since, were part of the colleges of Winchester and Eton. These two colleges together with the universities, were treated with special favour by King Henry VIII. In 1536 an Act was passed to ' exonerate ' them from the payment of First Fruits and Tenths, which had fallen to the revenues of the King. It is interesting to find in the Act itself the assurance of the King's ' fervent zeal for the increase of knowledge ' in the ' seven liberal sciences ' and the ' three tongues of Latin, Greek and Hebrew.' On this account he declares his desire to exempt the institutions named from the payments of First Fruits and Tenths ' lest it should perchance discourage many of his subjects, apt and willing to apply themselves to learning, and cause them by tenuity of living ' to go to other occupations. Hence Winchester and Eton amongst College Schools were saved from the *débâcle* of the dissolution of the ordinary non-University Colleges.

Winchester College buildings were finished in 1393, but in a Cathedral city the presumption is that the see, established in 676 A.D. would not have remained long without the provision of a Cathedral

---

[1] A. F. Leach: Article, ' Collegiate Church Schools ' in *Cyclopedia of Education* (edited by Paul Monroe), Vol. II, p. 112.

Grammar School. In Anglo-Saxon times, Asser the biographer of King Alfred mentions that the King sent one of his sons to a school at Winchester. The indications are, therefore, that Winchester College, was preceded by a Cathedral Grammar School, and that the institution of a grammar school in connexion with Winchester Cathedral had a more or less continuous existence from early Anglo-Saxon times.

The founder of Winchester College was William of Wykeham, one of the princely prelates of the Middle Ages, worthy forerunner of the better known Cardinal Wolsey. Nothing is more noteworthy in realising the significance of the history of grammar schools than the close association of all the developments with the greatest national figures of the time, whether prelates, statesmen, or private individuals. A history of England could well be written either from the material of the lives of the Founders, or from the lives of the pupils, thus showing the essentially national basis of the grammar school, however remote from national interests the curriculum and studies in the schools might *seem* to be, to the superficial investigator. Thus in the persons of Augustine, Theodore of Tarsus, Alcuin, King Alfred, Aelfric, Walter of Merton, Alexander Neckham, Richard of Bury—to say nothing of almost the whole of the bishops, who had an intimate connexion with education in their own Cathedral cities—the schools were

closely in touch with the national life and under the
direction of the national leaders.  And as the great
advances in the liberties of the people were constantly
associated with the bishops, so the educational progress was necessarily connected with ecclesiastical
dignitaries who had so often themselves risen from
the lowly ranks of the people, by the free and open
path made by the grammar schools.  Thus William of
Wykeham, most magnificent of prelates, was the son
of a stout yeoman, whose ancestors for generations,
'had ploughed the same lands, knelt at the same altar,
and paid due customs and service to the lord of the
manor.'  Let it not be forgotten that Wykeham was
a young man in the stirring times of the French wars.
Edward III on his return from the Battle of Crécy
and the capture of Calais in 1347, found the twenty-
three year old Wykeham living at Winchester,
'another Euclid,' as he seemed in geometry, steeped
in architectural skill, and abounding in ideas in
engineering.  He was of high service in the military
operations of the reign, and not less in the ecclesiastical works connected with St Stephen's, Westminster; and with Windsor Castle; and became clerk
and surveyor of the King's works.  The story goes
that envious mischief makers represented Wykeham
as placing the legend : 'This made Wykeham' on
the inner walls of Windsor Castle, suggesting that
the poor yeoman's son had intended to rob the King

of the honour of his castle by the assertion : ' Wykeham made this.'   But he replied :  ' I intended to
declare to the world that being intrusted with this
work "made" Wykeham.'   However, he rose to the
promulgation of a nobler legend than either of these
suggestions when he laid on all scholars of the
glorious foundation of Winchester College, on poor
and rich alike, the responsibility of showing that
' Manners maketh Man,' a dictum in its essential
truth as necessary for democratic as for aristocratic
education.

A true son of the Age of Chivalry, and of an age
which felt the inner necessity of rising to splendid
issues, whether in the wars of national expansion,
or in the glories of unique architectural enterprise
—all in the service of the one comprehensive and
cosmopolitan institution of the period, the Church—
Wykeham raised the noble buildings of Winchester
College—a school preceding Eton College in date—the
two sharing in the distinction of being the most
splendid of grammar schools.   For, as Mr Leach has
insisted, ' Public Schools' were originally grammar
schools.   Eton and Winchester Schools with a continuous history of six centuries (fully in the case of
Winchester and falling twenty years short of that
age in the case of Eton) are unique in England,
and (may we not say also ?) in Europe.   The
original foundation at Winchester was for a warden,

a headmaster, a second master, ten fellows, seventy scholars, three chaplains, three clerks, and sixteen choristers.

As if to vie with Winchester, and to assert the common interest of persons of high and low ancestral estate in this matter of the founding of schools, in 1440 (thirty-six years after Wykeham's death) King Henry VI followed the example of the yeoman's son, and erected a college at Eton, not less munificently planned than that of Winchester. The Royal Foundation was to be known as 'the College of the Blessed Marie of Etone beside Wyndsore' as the full title of Winchester College was 'Sainte Marie College of Wynchester.' Both founders, William of Wykeham and King Henry VI, associated their schools with the universities. Thus Wykeham built and endowed the beautiful New College, Oxford, to which Winchester boys should naturally proceed for higher studies, and similarly King Henry VI established King's College (and the majestic Chapel) in Cambridge, to which Eton 'sendeth annually her ripe fruit.' The method of association of grammar schools with colleges of the universities was afterwards often followed[1]. The Statutes of Eton were

[1] Christopher Wase in *Considerations Concerning Free Schools as settled in England* (1678) says: 'The connexion between Collegiate Schools and their correlative colleges conduces to their common good.'

modelled on those of Winchester. The King pur-
chased Eton parish church for his collegiate purposes.
Besides his letters patent, an Act of Parliament was
obtained for the college, and to crown all with the
highest ecclesiastical sanction, the King's efforts were
ratified, we may remember, by more than one Papal
bull. The college scheme provided for a provost, ten
fellows, four clerks, six choristers, a schoolmaster,
twenty-five poor and indigent scholars, and the same
number of poor, infirm men. In the course of its
history, as Sir H. C. Maxwell Lyte puts it, ' the School
has gradually risen to an unrivalled pitch of prosperity, and has practically monopolised the revenues
and the very name of Eton College.' Winchester
had its noble prelate in its founder's own person ;
Henry VI had at his side[1], as prompter and fellow
Maecenas, the puissant Cardinal Beaufort who, at
his death in 1447, left his money, valuable jewels
and relics to Eton College. He was a warrior,
and churchman, under whose guidance, and by
whose munificence, Winchester Cathedral was completed. He may be described as one of those
spirits, parallel in England to the Italian dukes, who
longed for many-sided fame, and in whom the
awakening of personality showed itself as it did in

[1] Soon after the foundation of Eton, a layman, William
de la Pole, afterwards Duke of Suffolk, surpassed everyone in
money gifts.

the Florentine dukes themselves.   Nor must we omit
to mention the Archbishop of Canterbury, Henry
Chichele, like William of Wykeham, the son of a
yeoman, who had led the ecclesiastical thanksgiving
for the great victory of Agincourt (1415) ; envoy to
France and encourager of Henry V in his war-policy,
but equally a supporter of learning in establishing
the Chichele Chest in Oxford University for poor
students, the founder of the splendid All Souls'
College, Oxford—and of special relevance to the
subject of this book as, still earlier, the founder of the
College Hospital and Grammar School at Higham
Ferrers in Northamptonshire in 1524, the school-
building being, until recently, still used as a school.
Small as this school is, and unimportant as its history
may be considered, it is of the same type and from
the same kind of warrior-prelate founders as Winchester and Eton.   Yet, gorgeous and noble as the
Eton College buildings were, they fell short of Henry
VI's intentions.   His plans included a church in the
pure Perpendicular style which should rank with the
very finest specimens of ecclesiastical architecture
in the country, excel Winchester Cathedral, and be
greater in size and dimensions than any church in
England except York Minster and the present
St Paul's Cathedral in London.   Such was the
provision for a worthy educational school-foundation
in the so-called ' Dark ' Ages !

One further name of a great prelate calls for notice even in a brief account of pre-Reformation grammar schools—William Waynflete the founder of Magdalen College, Oxford, with which he associated a school under a grammar-master. In 1429, Waynflete was master of Winchester College Grammar School, and in 1442, Henry VI secured him for the school at Eton, though in the next year he was placed in the provostship of Eton College. Waynflete afterwards became Bishop of Winchester and Lord Chancellor of England. In the Wars of the Roses naturally he was a Lancastrian, and on one occasion he released the unhappy Henry VI from his imprisonment in the Tower of London, though he afterwards acquiesced in the sovereignty of Edward IV and Richard III. Again in him we have a warrior-prelate. And again, we find, like Chichele at his birthplace of Higham Ferrers, Lord Chancellor Waynflete erected in 1484, a grammar school at his native village of Waynflete in Lincolnshire, which no doubt he intended as a seminary to his lordly Magdalen College at Oxford. His biographer, Chandler, describes the building in terms which take us back right into the atmosphere of the Middle Ages : ' All the windows of the school have been strongly ironed ; and those below have had very massive shutters on the outside, as appears from the iron hooks left in the wall. The civil war and the licence of the barons had rendered

precaution necessary.  It was unsafe to àbide in a
dwelling (there was the master's house within the
building) not barricaded or fortified.  A man's house
was indeed his castle.'

The very buildings, therefore, of the grammar
schools reflect the national life from age to age.  The
symbolism characteristic of the age, for instance,
affected the numbers fixed for the colleges.  Thus
altogether eleven in number at Winchester, the
Warden and Fellows represented the College of
Apostles, leaving out the traitor Judas.  The two
masters and the seventy scholars recalled the seventy-
two disciples according to the Vulgate.  The
two chaplains and three clerks alluded to the six
faithful deacons, omitting the apostate Nicholas.
The sixteen choristers represented the four greater
and twelve lesser prophets.  When Dean Colet
founded St Paul's School, London, he fixed the
number of pupils at 153 ' according to the number of
the fishes ' in the miraculous draught (St John
xxi. 11).

In the great changes that took place in the
country—the breaking up of the Feudal System, the
Black Death, the Reformation—the response to the
national disturbance was sensitively registered in the
schools.  The Acts of Dissolution, as we have seen,
destroyed many of the schools, and led to the re-
founding on a reduced scale of others.  But when the

fate of schools like Winchester and Eton had hung
in the balance, eventually inclining decisively to their
material prosperity, the inner changes were very
great. For instance, the Commissioners of Edward
VI, in 1547, determined for Winchester that the
Bible was to be read daily in hall, in English, that
the scholars were to buy the New Testament in
English or Latin and be regularly examined in it, that
the King's Primer (of orthodoxy) was to be studied,
—and that the warden and schoolmaster in ' all
lectures and lessons of profane authors, shall refute
and repel by allegation of Scriptures, all such
sentences and opinions as seem contrary to the Word
of God and Christian religion.'

Other requirements were negative as, for instance,
in the ceasing of prayers and hymns to the Virgin
Mary. The Commissioners included an injunction
which connects school history directly with the
revival of learning. Every scholar was to be required to possess and to study Erasmus' *Catechism*.
This Catechism, a remarkable production enough
in some of its large-minded interpretations of
Christianity, has been almost entirely passed by,
even by writers on Erasmus. The Commissioners'
Injunctions, to Winchester, of course, were upset,
in 1553, by the new régime of Queen Mary with her
Roman Catholicism ; and on the accession of Queen
Elizabeth, other and more distinctively Protestant

Catechisms than that of Erasmus were brought into use.

But, in spite of all the national changes of Anglo-Saxon, Norman, Medieval, Reformation times, the schools remained true to the idea of 'grammar' as an essential element in their continuity, even when overshadowed successively by logic, by mysticism, and, finally, by Protestant tenets.

Wykeham at Winchester directs that the seventy poor and needy scholars 'shall study and become proficient in grammaticals, in the art and science of grammar.' The master at Eton (*informator in grammatica* as he was called) was required definitely to instruct the twenty-five poor scholars, and also any other pupils from the realm of England who came there to learn grammar, and that without payment of any kind. Winchester and Eton are types of the other Collegiate Church Schools and the Chantries. 'Grammar' everywhere was regarded as the 'key to unlock the door of all knowledge,' or as Wykeham himself said, in his Statutes, it is 'the first of the liberal arts or sciences, the foundation, the door, and origin of all other liberal arts and sciences, for without it, the other arts and sciences could not exist in a completed form, nor could anyone attain fully any true knowledge in theory, or achievement in art.'

# CHAPTER IV

There is no event which more distinctly marks
off the medieval from the modern world than the
invention of printing ; and in no direction were
the effects of the introduction of printing of more
significance than in the grammar schools. It is
evident that the methods of teaching employed when
manuscript text-books were alone available could only
be oral. The teacher and the pupil had to rely on the
memory, the former often having to retain in his
memory the *verba ipsissima* of the authors he was
teaching, and perhaps of the grammar-text he taught.
There were varieties of grammar-texts in existence,
but these were largely handed down by tradition.
Even after the invention of printing the custom of oral
transmission still continued. A well-known instance
is that of John Stanbridge, Informator in Grammar
of Waynflete's Magdalen College (Oxford) Grammar
School and afterwards (1501) master of the Grammar School in connexion with the Hospital of St John
at Banbury. His methods of teaching were famous
throughout England. The Statutes of Manchester
Grammar School founded in 1515 required the
teaching of grammar ' according to the form of

grammar taught in the school of the town of Banbury.' There was a similar requirement at Cuckfield Grammar School and also at Merchant Taylors' School founded in 1560. Wimborne Grammar School (1509) was to follow the methods of Eton and Winchester and, later, the Master of Sevenoaks Grammar School, as re-founded in 1560, was to teach ' according to the methods used in the school of St Paul's in London.'

It must be borne in mind that through the easy multiplication of copies of the same text, it became much simpler for the Royal Authority to assert itself in the promulgation of uniform standards of authority in religion and education. In religion, the Book of Common Prayer, the King's Primer, and the order for the placing of Erasmus's Paraphrase in every parish church, are examples. In the address to the reader of the famous Lily's *Grammar* (*Brevissima Institutio, seu Ratio Grammatices cognoscendae*) in 1540, we are told : ' As his Majesty purposeth to establish his people in one consent and harmony of pure and true religion ; so his tender goodness toward the youth and childhood of his realm, intendeth to have it brought up under one absolute and uniform sort of learning. For his Majesty, considering the great encumbrance and confusion of the young and tender wits by reason of the diversity of grammar rules and teachings, (for heretofore every master had his grammar and every school divers teachings, and changing of masters and schools did many times utterly dull and undo good wits),' had one grammar (Lily's) prepared, and he made its use compulsory on all grammar schools by his Royal Proclamation. Edward VI's and Queen Elizabeth's Injunctions continued the re- -quirement that none other grammar ' shall be taught in any school or other place within the King's realms and dominions, but only that which is set forth by the said authority.' The Canons ecclesiastical of 1604 established the authorisation of Lily's Grammar, and presumably the requirement is still in force. In 1758 Lily's Grammar was ' transformed and appropriated ' as the Eton Latin Grammar, and this recognition was continued till 1868, when in the headmastership of Dr Hornby, it was superseded. The introduction of printing thus provided the facilities which an absolute Tudor monarchy was more than ready to seize upon, in establishing its external authority over the grammar schools. In the internal arrangements of the schools, it was one of the main causes of the change from the oral instruction of the Medieval Ages, to the written paper-work of exercises, composition, and theses, which prevailed in the Tudor, Stuart, and later times, down to our own days.

After the introduction of printing, amongst the

great national changes, came the Protestant Reformation. We have seen that the first Cathedral educational scheme included more than a score of special foundations or re-foundations, and that these, through the financial filchings of kings and courtiers, were reduced to the Six New Foundations, as they are termed, of Henry VIII. In Cranmer's mind, at least, we know that there was the idea that from the abbey lands also grammar schools should have been founded ' in *every shire of England, where children most apt* to learning, should have been brought up freely, and without great cost to their friends and kinsfolk.'

Thus was lost the great opportunity for grammar schools. The Reformation period started with the throwback of a great thinning of the old schools, and the problem presented itself : How could the Protestant religion, which founded itself on the Bible, secure the reading of it at least in the vernacular, and if possible, a knowledge of the text in Latin, Greek and Hebrew for a reasonable number of expert protagonists against Catholic scholars? Here was a complex problem, becoming more and more urgent as the political exigencies identified the national policy with the Protestant cause. Never, before or since, was it more necessary that the grammar schools should be the expression of the nation's best culture, cast in the mould of the national

Church. During the Tudor period, from the point of view of the schools, State and Church were one, and the schools, while feeling the domination of both, at least could respond to both, for the antagonistic element, viz. the Roman Catholic schoolmasters, was excluded by pains and penalties, of the direst kind, from introducing a disturbing element into the school system.

The large number of schools called by the name of Henry VIII and of Edward VI, it is true, were not founded by them, in the sense of being established by those monarchs in the places where schools previously had not existed, or from funds which they personally supplied. But the names bear witness to the national necessity of a supply of schools with which the Kings wished to identify themselves, at least by having an easily earned credit for their association with them. Henry V, as Stow tells us, suppressed certain ' Priories alien and Hospitals ' in London, and from the funds Henry VI appointed by letters patent that grammar schools should be established in London, at St Paul's, St Martin's-le-Grand, St Mary-le-Bow-in-Cheap, St Dunstan's-in-the-West and St Anthony's, where we have seen Colet was educated, and we may add, Sir Thomas More and afterwards Archbishop Whitgift. So that Henry VIII's spoliation of hospitals and their schools, was a continuation on a large scale of what had obtained before, but Henry VI's name is not associated with his re-foundation as closely as Henry VIII's with his, simply because the former's acts were rather individualistic, whilst Henry VIII's and Edward VI's were identified with the national policy laid down by ecclesiastics like Cranmer, and such laymen as Somerset, Mildmay, and Rich.

The demand for the provision of grammar schools shows an apparent educational enthusiasm, but it was largely the desire to supply the place of the older dissolved schools. Thomas Lever, the master of St John's College, Cambridge, preached boldly before the King (Edward VI) on the 'most miserable drowning of youth in ignorance,' by the closing of old schools, and Martin Bucer, one of the trusted foreign protestants in England, adviser and colleague to Cranmer and the Protector Somerset in the changes to Protestantism, urged on the King the duty of making education the care of the State. Hugh Latimer, Bishop of Worcester, told how his father a 'yeoman' had 'kept me to school,' how in the past, rich men had constantly left money to help poor scholars, and he pleads ' let *us* maintain schools and scholars,' and again he declared : ' they that do somewhat for the furtherance of learning, for maintaining of schools and scholars, they sanctify God's holy name.' The necessity of education was recognised, and the re-foundation of Edward VI's

grammar schools is the outward expression of the
demand of that increasingly powerful section of the
community, which had fallen under the influence of
the combined forces of the Renascence and the
Protestant Reformation.  Private individuals joined
in the foundation of schools.  The spirit which led
rich men to endow by will chantries in their own
parish-church, and to make provision for the chantry
priest to teach grammar in it, gave way, in the
Protestant scheme of public life, to the foundation
or further endowment of a grammar school, in
the successful man's birthplace.  The rise of the
great merchant class, members of powerful trade-
guilds, had given the impulse to this willingness to
help education, as the source of national prosperity,
before the Reformation, and the tendency was
strengthened by that change, and of course, especially
deepened in the directions which the new theology
developed.

Stow in his *Survey of London* (1603), the last year
of Queen Elizabeth's reign, gives an interesting list
of citizens of London who had founded grammar
schools in the town or county in which they were
born.  This list includes Sir John Percivall, Merchant
Taylor of London, who founded in 1498 a grammar
school at Macclesfield, and his wife, Lady Thomasine,
foundress of a grammar school at St Mary Wike in
Cornwall, her birthplace; Stephen Gennings, Merchant

Taylor, who founded a school at Wolverhampton in
1509; John Tate, brewer and mercer, a Free School
near St Anthony's; George Monoux, draper, at
Walthamstow 1515; Sir William Laxton, grocer, at
Oundle 1545; Sir John Gresham, mercer, at Holt in
Norfolk 1548; Sir Rowland Hill, mercer, at Drayton
in Shropshire; Sir Andrew Judd, skinner, at Ton-
bridge in Kent in 1551; Sir Thomas White, Merchant
Taylor, founded St John's College, Oxford in 1554;
William Harper founded his grammar school at
Bedford in 1562; Sir Thomas Gresham, mercer,
founded Gresham College in 1566; Sir Wolstan
Dixie, skinner, the grammar school at Market
Bosworth in 1586. Stow might have added—John
Royse, mercer, at Abingdon in 1562; W. Parker,
woollen draper, at Daventry in 1576; John Fox,
goldsmith, at Dean in Cumberland in 1596; Richard
Platt, brewer, at Aldenham in 1597; and those still
better known examples of Lawrence Sheriff, grocer,
at Rugby in 1567, and Peter Blundell the merchant
and manufacturer in the kersey trade, who founded
the interesting grammar school at Tiverton in 1599.

Yeomen have played no unimportant part in
the earlier educational progress, and are an interesting class. We have seen the position which
yeomen's sons had reached in the case of Wykeham,
Chichele and Hugh Latimer. Though Lawrence
Sheriff, founder of Rugby, was himself a grocer,

his father probably was a yeoman at Brownsover
near Rugby. But of yeomen, it is not often easy
to find biographies. Of John Lyon, the founder of
Harrow School, almost all that is known is to be
found in the inscription on his tombstone, ' Here
lieth buried the body of John Lyon, late of Preston,
in this parish, yeoman, deceased 11 October, in the
year of our Lord 1592 ; who hath founded a free
grammar school in the parish to have continuance
for ever, and for maintenance thereof, and for relief
of the poor, and of some poor scholars in the Universities, repairing of highways, and other good and
charitable uses, hath made conveyance of lands of
good value to a corporation granted for that purpose.
Praise be to the author of all goodness, who makes us
mindful to follow his good example.' John Harrox,
yeoman, of Moulton in Lincolnshire, in 1560, be-
queathed by will, provision for a grammar school in
that parish to be erected and kept for ever, after his
decease, ' in the mansion-house ' in which he had
lived. The county grammar school of Holt, in
Norfolk, was similarly the ' mansion-house ' of Sir
John Gresham mentioned above, converted into a
school, from which small school it is said that within
two hundred years to one college alone, above eighty
boys went, of whom seven were elected fellows and
one rose to be master of the college.

In addition to the successful merchants like

Gresham, on their return to their native villages and towns, and to the yeomen who never left their homes in search of riches or adventure, noblemen and country gentlemen founded schools. Shakespeare refers to one instance in the play of *King Henry VI, Part ii*, Act iv, Sc. 7, l. 37, where Jack Cade says to Lord Saye and Sele: ' Thou hast most traitorously corrupted the youth of the realm in erecting a grammar school ; and, whereas, before, our forefathers had no other books but the score and the tally, thou hast caused printing to be used, and contrary to the King, his crown and dignity, thou hast built a paper-mill. It will be proved to thy face that thou hast men about thee that usually talk of a noun and a verb, and such abominable words as no Christian can endure to hear.' The attack on grammar schools put into Cade's mouth certainly represents the attitude of the authorities against the schools in the early 15th century in the attempt to extirpate Lollardry. Lord Saye and Sele died in 1450.

Grammar schools undoubtedly appealed then as always to the more cultured classes in the community though there was no institution which did so much to aid the humbler classes to rise in the social scale, when they had the ability to profit by school-education, for the grammar school exacted very moderate fees, if any at all.

But highly important as the influence of kings,

merchants, noblemen and gentlemen, was in endowing and supporting individual schools, the directive energies of the working clergy, of theologians, and of divines were even more potent when we remember their two-fold relation to grammar schools, viz. as founders and also as dominating the religious cast of the work of the schools, in the curriculum, and ' atmosphere ' of schoolwork. It is not merely to the early Reformation we turn for illustration. After the days of Henry VIII and Edward VI the policy of cherishing schools was as carefully continued by Cardinal Pole in desire at any rate, as by Cranmer, and in Queen Mary's reign, royal refoundations of schools continued as they had begun in Henry VIII's and Edward VI's reigns. Cardinal Pole was a humanist, and though intent on reestablishing the old ecclesiastical system he was a friend to learning. Queen Mary herself founded five grammar schools, and as many as fifteen schools were established by private individuals. But in the later Reformation, that of Queen Elizabeth, when the Anglican Church came to its definite settlement, the ecclesiastical and doctrinal colour of the tendencies of the national settlement were firmly stamped upon the schools.

It was inevitable that this should be so. The real directors of the polity and doctrine of the Elizabethan Church were the clergy, who in Queen

Mary's reign had suffered voluntary exile abroad rather than recant their Protestantism, or run the risk of the same fate as met the stalwart defenders of the Protestant faith in the fires of Smithfield. From the time of Edward VI's Prayer Book of 1552, when Peter Martyr and John à Lasco had helped to bring Cranmer to a modification of views in the direction of the Zwinglian school of Swiss reformers, England was drawn nearer to the followers of Calvin than to the Lutherans. From the beginning or soon after the beginning of Mary's reign, 1553, till the accession of Queen Elizabeth in 1558, groups of English exiles fled from the persecutions. The Lutherans in Germany gave the English refugees the cold shoulder, whilst they were warmly welcomed by the towns of Emden in East Friesland, Wesel bordering on the Low Countries, Aarau near Berne, Strassburg, Zurich, Frankfort on the Main, and Geneva. With all their differences they were all drawn together under the spell of Calvin or Zwingli, rather than by Lutherans. This close association of the English exiles with the Swiss divines, their co-religionists, in a common revolt against Roman Catholicism, was of signal importance in bringing the English Elizabethan Church into the theological atmosphere of Zurich and Geneva. The English refugees almost, if not entirely, identified themselves with an attitude towards religion which naturally grew into the Puritanism of the reign of Elizabeth, and in the following century developed a severely theocratic type. The consequences of the residence, during critical years, of the English refugees in these foreign cities of exile, cannot easily be over-estimated in the results, not only to the course of English religion, but also to that of English educational history. On the whole, educational history in England up to this time had been isolated. England had been subjected to Papal decrees, and had been submerged first in the Anglo-Saxon and secondly in the Norman-French introduction of foreign ideas of culture ; but our country had not been drawn into the full current of European culture and thought of the Renascence and the Reformation. Nothing like such an exodus of those who were to become among the best of the English thinking and working clergy and laity, had ever taken place. For although happily individual nobles and scholars had gone to study in Padua, in Florence, in Rome, in Ferrara and in other cities of Italy, they were comparatively few in number, whereas the English religious exiles went in groups, received new impressions in common association, and under the stern conditions of relating all new experiences to the central principles of religious inquiry and conviction. The English Reformers who went into exile in Queen Mary's reign were co-religionists, more or less, of their foreign scholarly

friends, but they were also observers, in a highly
favourable attitude of mind for learning from new
surroundings, of the habits, customs, and institutions,
presented before their eyes.   For all the rest of their
lives, on their return to England, they drew, from the
store-house of their memories, vivid reminiscences of
their foreign experience for precept, and for example.
In the educational domain the Calvinistic influence
was almost electrical.   John Calvin and his co-
adjutors had transformed a city by education.   When
Robert Owen, in the early 19th century, affirmed that
' any character may be given to any community in
the world by the application of proper means,' he
might have pointed to the city of Geneva under the
sway of Calvin, as absolute as that of any Tudor
monarch, though with the prophet's moral and
religious fervour behind him.   Nor will any one doubt
the all-compelling influence of the Calvinist atmos-
sphere in Geneva, not only in civic relations, but
also in direct school organisation and school aims, if
he recalls the fact that from that origin came the
Dutch system of schools, and nearer England, the
Scotch system of grammar schools and of elementary education, far more thoroughly devised and
methodically administered than in England, a system
evolved by the powerful mind of John Knox, the
religious and no less educational reformer, the disciple
of John Calvin in education as well as in religion.   For

it was from the *Book of Discipline* drawn up by Knox, that we must trace the origin of the later legislative system, which provided Scotland with its organisation of secondary as well as of elementary education.

Although Calvin was the greatest of the foreign reformers, whom the English exiles met, yet there were others of no mean 'intellectual light and leading,' *e.g.* Theodore Beza, Heinrich Bullinger, Rudolph Gualter, Wolfgang Musculus, Peter Martyr Vermigli, Pierre Viret, and though John Knox had been in England, yet he was to most of the exiles a new as well as a strong personality, who must have counted greatly with the Englishmen as a factor in directions of active and reactive educational influence.

Once more, we shall see that the history of the grammar schools runs, if not *pari passu*, at any rate closely after, and in direct connexion with, national changes. Let us recall the names of some of the English religious exiles of Mary's reign, who returned with the accession of Queen Elizabeth, strengthened by their foreign friends in convictions ingrained by common enthusiasms, developed amid self-sacrifices, hardships and biting poverty, a set of men to whom we might be sure that England would owe much, even if we did not know that the depth and intensity of later Puritanism are only explained as the fruit of the mental and moral struggles of the exiles, and the earlier national tragedy of the fires of Smithfield.

# CHAPTER V

If we recall the names of some of the chief of the English foreign exiles who returned to England, and the posts which they occupied, we shall see the opportunities which they had for influencing the whole tenour of the higher religious, moral and educational changes of the brilliant epoch of Elizabeth's reign, and we can then turn to the educational work accomplished by some of them, individually, in connexion with grammar schools.

There were two future Archbishops in exile at Strassburg, Edmund Grindal, who afterwards was master of Pembroke Hall, Cambridge, 1558–61, Archbishop of Canterbury, 1575, on the death of Parker; and Edwin Sandys, afterwards Archbishop of York, 1576–88, both of whom founded schools. Grindal established in 1583 the grammar school at St Bees in Cumberland, in which township he was born. The Statutes drawn up by Grindal are interesting and full. He requires that the master 'shall carefully seek to bring up all his scholars equally in learning and good manners,' and 'he shall chiefly labour to make his scholars profit in the Latin and Greek grammar, and to the end that they may the better profit therein he shall exercise

them in the best authors in both tongues that are
mete for their capacity.' But he goes on to say,
' provided always that the first books of instruction
that they shall read either in Latin or Greek shall be
the smaller Catechisms set forth by public authority
for that purpose in the said tongues, which we will
that they shall learn by heart, that with the knowledge of the tongues they may also learn their duty
towards God and man.' Similarly Archbishop
Sandys founded a grammar school at Hawkshead, in
Lancashire. The schoolmaster, by Sandys' statutes,
was to teach grammar and the principles of the
Greek tongue, with ' other sciences necessary to be
taught in a grammar school.' Both the master and
the usher were required to ' teach all such good
authors which do contain honest precepts of virtue,
and good literature, for the better education of
youth ; and shall once every week, at least, instruct
and examine his scholars in the principles of true
religion.' Grindal's predecessor in the Archbishop-
ric of Canterbury, Matthew Parker (1559–75) was
not an exile ; he had lived ' privately ' and ' by
shifting from place to place ' in England had escaped
a martyr's death in Mary's reign. Parker, however,
was identified with the educational activities of the
returned exiles, as may be seen in the case of his
foundation of the Rochdale Grammar School in 1564
for the youth of the parish, free of cost, ' that they

might be brought up in the learning of true piety
and the Latin tongue.' Parker asked the 'sanction
of the names' of Richard Cox, once tutor of
Edward VI, and at one time headmaster of Eton,
who had been an exile at Frankfort, of Robert Horne,
who had been chief minister of the exiles at Frankfort,
and on his return chosen as bishop of Winchester
(1564–80), of Thomas Watts, also an exile at Frankfort, and afterwards Archdeacon of Middlesex, and
of Alexander Nowell, dean of St Paul's, who all
subscribed Parker's original scheme of endowment
and were present also at the delivery of the school
charter and title-deeds to James Wouldsenden,
clothier, and John Warbarton, merchant, both of
Rochdale, proxies for the parish, 1571. Dean Nowell
had been headmaster of Westminster School from
1543 to the death of Edward VI. He had also been an
exile at Frankfort. Afterwards, on the death of his
brother Robert, he carried out the latter's injunction :
' Forget not Middleton School and the College of
Brasenose, where we were brought up in our youth,'
and endowed at the same time the Free School at
Middleton and thirteen scholarships at Brasenose
College. Robert Nowell, who had accumulated a
fortune as Attorney General of the Court of Wards,
left the disposal of his money to the Dean, who
devoted very large amounts, in the total, in grants
to poor scholars in the universities and to poor

scholars in ' divers grammar schools.' Amongst
the ' scholars ' thus benefited by Nowell were
Edmund   Spenser,   Richard   Hooker,   Launcelot
Andrewes, and Richard Hakluyt. The Skinners'
Company, in whose hands Sir Andrew Judd had
placed the management of the Free Grammar School
of Tonbridge, submitted their ' rules and orders ' to
Nowell, for advice.   One of the original rules was
that ' no remedy for playe ' should be allowed ' above
ffower tymes in the yeare.'   The good Dean, who,
though he had learned much from the Swiss Calvinism,
still had enough of the milk of human kindness
towards boys, placed a note in the margin of the document: 'Leave to play once a week may well be borne
with.'  Nowell seems, further, to have disemburdened
his educational soul, by the statutes which he provided for the re-foundation of the Friars' School,
Bangor, by Dr Geoffrey Glỳnne in 1561, in which the
Genevan influence is seen in the clearest fashion.
Dean Nowell's influence on English grammar school
education was profound, similar to that of Melanch-
thon in Germany, and he might be called the consultant-educationist of Elizabethan England.   Thus,
when there was reasonable doubt as to the appointment of a man named Anthony Rushe to the headmastership of the King's School, Canterbury, Dean
Wotton of Canterbury wrote to Archbishop Parker
suggesting that Dr Nowell should be consulted as to

the appointment. From 1560 to 1602 Nowell was
Dean of St Paul's, and besides his Mentor-like attitude to all grammar school concerns, he wrote the
standard, authorised school Catechism, to be further
mentioned in the next chapter.

The Dean of Westminster from 1560 to 1601 contemporary with Nowell as Dean of St Paul's, was
Gabriel Goodman who apparently drew up the
curriculum of Westminster School, after the model
of Eton, though with more emphasis on Greek.
Goodman was not one of the exiles, and the religious
observations, we are not surprised to find, are more
after the medieval fashion of schools than in line with
the Genevan models. One of the exercises introduced was the reading aloud of old Latin manuscripts
'to facilitate the reading of such hands.' Dean
Goodman obtained a perpetual grant of a house
attached to the prebend of Chiswick as a place of
refuge for the members of the Chapter and College
whenever pestilence was raging in Westminster, and
in the later summer months, the College removed to
that house for a change. This College house in later
times became the office of the famous Chiswick Press.
Goodman's successor was ' that most rare preacher '
Launcelot Andrewes (pupil of Richard Mulcaster,
first headmaster of the Merchant Taylors' School,
1561–86) who not only in his ' retirements ' to
Chiswick ' always took two scholars with him,'

but also at his own study in his house at Westminster in the evenings would send for the Upper
Form 'and teach them Greek and Hebrew.' He
would also teach in the school itself, it is said, for
a week together.

To return to the ' exiles.' Miles Coverdale, the
well-known translator of the Bible, not only was an
exile in 1554–59, but he had also previously visited
Protestant Germany and had been pastor and schoolmaster at Bergzabern in Deux Ponts from 1543 to
1547 under the name of Michael Anglus. From 1551
to 1553 he had been bishop of Exeter. John Jewel,
afterwards bishop of Salisbury, religious exile at
Frankfort, Strassburg and Zurich, was Reader in
Humanity and Rhetoric at Corpus Christi College,
Oxford, for seven years and was accustomed himself to
'write something every day,' and proclaimed to all as
his educational maxim : ' men acquire more learning
by the frequent exercise of the pen than by reading
many books,' a maxim which became a practice at any
rate in some grammar schools. In accordance with
what was probably an ancient episcopal custom
(followed to some degree, as we have seen, by Dean
Andrewes), 'perceiving the great want of learned men
he took care to have six poor lads constantly in his
house, whom he educated under his own eye carefully,
directing them in the pursuit of their studies : and he
took no small delight in hearing them dispute on

points of critical and grammatical knowledge in the
dead languages at his table during their meals; often
setting them right, or enlarging their views on the
subject in question.' This illustration throws light
upon the origin of private grammar schools.

Jewel's biographer was Laurence Humphrey,
an exile at Zurich, and one of the learned Calvinists.
He became President of Magdalen College, Oxford,
1561–90. His influence on the age was very great.
He wrote a book for the guidance of the young noble.
"The fine of their whole study is first to know God,
next themselves, to govern well their family, the
state.' ' Of catechisms and institutions of Christian
religion,' said Humphrey, ' the chief of our age is
John Calvin's.'

Two other bishops—returned exiles (one at Zurich
the second at Frankfort)—viz. John Parkhurst,
bishop of Norwich (1560–75) and James Pilkington,
bishop of Durham (1561–76) took close care of
educational interests. Parkhurst admitted no one
to preaching ' that had no knowledge in the Latin
tongue.' Pilkington founded a grammar school in
1566, at Rivington, in Lancashire. His statutes for
the school are amongst the most graphic we have,
as showing the methods for acquiring Latin vocabularies, the grading of the authors read, and
especially the written exercises to be required from
scholars. ' Perfection,' he says, speaking of younger

children under the usher's care, ' is not to be looked
for in these young years, nor in these grammar rules,
but rather in observation, noting and learning how
the best Latin writers have used to speak.' Daily
exercise in Latin speaking must be required. Like
the rest of the returned exiles, in the schools that
came under their guidance, religious exercises are
strictly laid down. ' The usher shall exercise his
younger sort in learning their short catechism in
English in the Common Book [*i.e.* Book of Common
Prayer], and to all sorts, the master shall read
Mr Nowell's, or Calvin's Catechism, taught in Calvin's
*Institutions*, willing the elder sort both to learn it
by heart, and examine them briefly the next day
after, when they come to school again, before they
go to other things, how they can say it, and shall
commend them that have done well, and encourage
others to do the like.'

The Elizabethan bishop of St David's, Richard
Davies, was a returned exile from Geneva, who
did for Wales, educationally, what Pilkington and
Parkhurst were doing in England. Davies was one of
the founders of the Grammar School at Carmarthen.
The others concerned in the foundation were Walter
Devereux, Earl of Essex, Sir James Crofft, Griffin
Rece, Walter Vaughan of Golden Grove, and
Robert Toye. The bishop translated the Prayer
Book into Welsh and also collaborated with William

Salesbury in the first translation into Welsh of the
New Testament. Both were issued in 1567. The
Genevan influence therefore was directly felt in
Welsh education.

Bernard Gilpin, 'that patriarchial divine' as
Thomas Fuller called him, was not a bishop but the
country rector of Houghton-le-Spring in Durham.
He had been begged to accept the bishopric of
Carlisle, but had absolutely declined promotion,
preferring to be an 'apostle of the North' of England
generally, to being limited to a diocese. He had
travelled in the Low Countries and was deeply
concerned at the ignorance of the North of England.
It is probable he had devised a grammar school
for Houghton-le-Spring before his friend Bishop
Pilkington had obtained the letters patent for his
school at Rivington in 1566. After the manner of
the pre-Reformation foundations, (followed by some
later founders, *e.g.* Archbishop Whitgift at Croydon
and Bishop Abbot at Guildford) he planned the
gift of a grammar school together with almshouses
which were added later. The original statutes of
Houghton-le-Spring are not to be found, but since
Gilpin revised those of his friend Pilkington, for
Rivington, they were probably very similar. From
later statutes of Houghton (probably founded on
Gilpin's) we find it was enacted that there should be
school prayers, and every scholar was to have a copy

of them sewed into his grammar. The master's
' principal regard shall be ' that his scholars frequent
divine service on holy days ' with godly books to
look on,' and to help them to do this, ' he shall read
to them the Catechism, Greek and Latin, appointed
for all schools, teaching them in discourse of their
lessons their duty towards God, their parents, and
all others.' Like Bishop Jewel, he often had the
promising scholars in his study at the rectory and
gave them lessons himself. Many of the scholars
were boarders, and of these a considerable number
were boarded, clothed and educated at Gilpin's own
expense. When the numbers increased so that
suitable accommodation could not be got for boarders
in the village, Gilpin received boys into his own house,
and often had as many as twenty living with him,
only accepting payment for board from sons of the
well-to-do, knights and squires ; from many of the
others asking nothing. He sought out promising
boys to add to the numbers of the well-educated.

Near to Gilpin and Houghton-le-Spring was
William Whittingham, dean of Durham, another
returned exile from Frankfort. He had not actually
founded a grammar school, but, as a Swiss traveller,
he recognised the claims of educational interest in
his daily duties. He describes his connexion with
the Cathedral Grammar School at Durham (one of
those re-foundations of Henry VIII) : ' First in the

morning at six of the clock, the Grammar School
and Song School, with all the servants of the House,
resort to Prayers into the Church : which exercise
continueth almost half an hour....Because we lack
an able schoolmaster, *I bestow daily three or four hours
in teaching the youth.*'

Others of the clergy founded schools. Archdeacon
Richard Johnson provided and endowed two grammar schools, those at Oakham and Uppingham.
Johnson was too young in Queen Mary's reign to
get involved in the religious controversies, but he
had travelled abroad for three years in Queen
Elizabeth's reign. He was chaplain at Gorhambury
to Sir Nicholas Bacon, and was a decided Puritan.
The story of the education of his son is remarkable.
The boy is said to have read over the Hebrew Bible,
and to have been able to speak Latin, Greek and
Hebrew, French, Italian, Spanish, and to have
been also able to write in each. The story can at
any rate be accepted as an indication of width of
educational aims in some of the founders who had
met and mixed with foreign educationists.

The same spirit of *pietas literata* animated the
lesser dignitaries of the Church, who had returned
from Swiss exile. Thomas Becon, for example, who
had professed Protestantism, had been obliged to
recant, and supported himself by teaching. He had
been chaplain to Cranmer and rector of St Stephen

Walbrook in 1547, fléd to Strassburg in 1554, and on his return to England was restored to his old benefice. He gives the Genevan view of the schoolmaster, who ' shall gather such flowers out of the holy Bible for his scholars, with the sweet and strong savor whereof they may repel and put away the pestiferous and mortal odours of the errors and heresies not only of the papists, but also of all other sectaries....So teach the poets, orators, historiographers, philosophers, etc., not that they should be mates with God's word but rather handmaids unto it, and serve to set forth the honour and glory thereof.'

To Thomas Becon, belongs the distinction of being the first, in England, to demand the establishment of girls' schools ' in letters and manners ' as well as of boys' grammar schools. The following is a striking passage and must not be passed by in a history of grammar schools. It shows that the returned exiles had been stirred to think freely and independently on educational problems, by their residence abroad :

' If it be thought convenient, as it is most convenient, that schools should be erected and set up for the right education and bringing up of the youth of the male kind, why should it not be thought convenient that schools be built for the godly institution and virtuous bringing up of the youth of the female kind ? Is not the woman the creature

of God as well as the man, and as dear unto God as
the man ? Is not the woman a necessary member
of the commonweal ? Have not we all our beginning
of her ? Are we not born, nursed, and brought up
of a woman ? Do not the children for the most part
prove even such as the mothers are of whom they
come ? Can the mothers bring up their children
virtuously, when they themselves be void of all
virtue ? Can the nurses instil any goodness into the
tender breasts of their nurse-children, when they
themselves have learned none ? Can that woman
govern her house godly which knoweth not one point
of godliness ? Who seeth not now then, how necessary the virtuous education and bringing-up of the
woman-kind is ? Which thing cannot be conveniently
brought to pass, except schools for that purpose be
appointed, and certain godly matrons ordained
governesses of the same, to bring up the maids and
young women in the doctrine and nurture of the
Lord. And verily, in my judgment, they do no
less deserve well of the Christian commonweal,
that found and stablish schools with honest stipends
for the education and bringing up of the women-
children in godliness and virtue than they which
erect and set up schools for the instruction of the
men-children in good letters and godly manners.'

One of the most remarkable educational claims
of the Reformation period, the passage occurs in an

apparently solely religious manual called *A New Catechism*, written about the middle of the 16th century or a little later.


CHAPTER VI

CHURCH CONTROL OF THE GRAMMAR SCHOOLS

The medieval Church entering into the ideal of the old Roman empire, desired universality, and perpetuity. The direction of education was a logical means to this end. With the unique organisation which the Church possessed, there was great advantage for education, as far as the extension of schools was concerned. But for a great portion of the Middle Ages, it meant that all access to professional careers, in law and physic as well as in theology, was ecclesiastic, and as the Church organisation rested itself on Aristotelian scholasticism, professional and secular knowledge could not easily win its emancipation from the ecclesiastical standard. A point of considerable importance to note is that the Church realised that to control the teachers was to control the schools. Accordingly the Church took upon itself the provision and the licensing of teachers. Thus in 826 Pope Eugenius declared that it was the duty of bishops to establish masters and teachers

in suitable places.  In 1179, the Third Lateran Council
ordered every Cathedral to provide a master with
a benefice, so that he might teach the clerks of the
Church and the other poor students *gratis*.  The
Fourth Lateran Council not only required every Cathedral Church, but every other Church whose finance
permitted it, to appoint a competent master to teach
grammar *gratis* to the clerks of the Church, and every
archiepiscopal Church to have a theological teacher
to whom a prebend should be allotted.  Such
decrees were drawn up for all Europe.  And in 1200
A.D. the Council of Westminster prescribed for
England that the relatives of priests might claim
instruction from the churches and that priests were
to teach schools in their towns and give instruction
*gratis* to any children whom any devout person
wished to place with them.  More remarkable is
the provision that priests ought always to have a
school of schoolmasters in their houses (Presbyteri
semper debent in domibus suis ludimagistrorum
scholas habere).

The medieval grammar schools were thus chiefly
grouped around the Cathedrals and (though some were
placed under Abbeys) directly under the supervision
of the bishop.  In the same way that the Church
had a monopoly of the schools it claimed complete
control over the teachers.  No one could teach without the 'licence' of the Ordinary of the diocese

(*i.e.* the bishop or the officer acting for him). Mr Leach has included in his *Educational Charters*, p. 91, the first instance known of a writ from the acting Bishop of London, *c.* 1138 A.D. threatening excommunication to any man who should dare to teach without the licence of the schoolmaster of St Paul's Cathedral, *i.e.* acting as delegate of the Bishop. In his account of Beverley Grammar School, Mr Leach has given a full description of actual excommunication of a rival schoolmaster by the Chapter of Beverley though on relinquishing his school he was absolved. The Council at Westminster, 1200 A.D., required that no charge should be made for licences to schoolmasters, and if such had been actually paid, the money was to be refunded. The application for a licence did not necessitate the schoolmaster being a priest, and there is sufficient evidence that medieval licensed schoolmasters were not all priests—but, as Mr de Montmorency says, 'it does assert the all-controlling power of the Church over education.' The same writer has made it clear that though such action as the Beverley case was good by Canon Law of the Church, the Gloucester Grammar School case in 1410 proved that by the Common Law of England no action could lie against a rival non-licensed schoolmaster for damage, as for instance, by causing fees for tuition to be lowered all round. It was decided that ' to teach youth

is a virtuous and charitable thing to do and helpful to
the people for which a man cannot be punished by
our law.' The Canon Law could and did punish
schoolmasters who set up school independently of
the masters to whom the Church had granted the
monopoly ; as early as 1410, it was decided in the
Court of Common Pleas that the Common Law of
the Realm declined to intervene. And yet, for
three centuries after this date, as Mr de Montmorency says ' the Church amid its marvellous vicissi-
tudes never relaxed its hold on the control of the
teaching of youth and treated as dead or non-
existent the sleeping though living doctrine of the
Common Law.'

For, when the Church, in England, changed its
views from Romanism to Protestantism, and the
headship of the Church passed from the Pope to
the King, the continuity of its claim to control
education was unaffected. In some degree, indeed,
it seemed desirable to tighten its grip. For with
a new set of doctrines to maintain, grounded on a
historical book, the Bible, the work of education
received a new impetus. Personal salvation, in a
sense, depended, indirectly at least, on the power of
reading, which thus became a necessity of education
for religion's sake, and if we may add that some
degree of power of interpretation was also necessary
as part of the demand for the exercise of private

judgment, a trained educated mind was also, inferentially, essential. But still more urgent was the argument that for Protestants to hold their own in discussion with Catholics, the concept of education must be deepened in intension and widened in extension to a degree, hitherto unnecessary, in ages of accepted uniformity of creed. It is true that the Lollards had endeavoured to extend and to improve education, for this very reason, but they had been suppressed, and the uniformity upon which the Catholics had insisted in the 15th century, the Protestants endeavoured in their turn to get by suppression of Catholic education, and at the same time to secure improvement in that of their own children. With these aims in the background, all the machinery of the splendid organisation of the old church was at the royal service and utilised to the full by the Kings, Henry VIII and Edward VI, and by Queen Elizabeth. Some of their proceedings showing their use of the control of schools may now be briefly sketched.

For the most part the educational requirements of the post-Reformation ecclesiastical authorities were in continuity with the medieval practice, or had some points of similarity with it. Thus, when King Henry VIII issued his Royal Proclamation authorising Lily's *Grammar* as the only Grammar to be used in schools, he was not acting merely in

an autocratic manner, for in 1529 the Convocation
of Canterbury had prescribed for that province what
the Royal Proclamation of 1540 made general for
the kingdom.  Convocation had urged that through
the outbreak of plague in the towns in which
grammar schools were situated, or through the
death of a master and a new master's predilections,
it often happened that boys suffered greatly by
changes in the grammars used.  Convocation, therefore, proposed a uniform method of teaching and a
uniform grammar, to be prescribed the following year
by a committee consisting of the Archbishop, four
other bishops of the province, four abbots and four
archdeacons.  In 1540, King Henry VIII had
caused ' sundry learned men,' amongst whom was
Dr Richard Cox already mentioned (at one time headmaster of Eton, at another tutor to King Edward VI,
on the Commission also for drawing up the English
Liturgy, and a former 'exile' at Frankfort), to
reduce the former attempts 'in this kind' into one
' body of Grammar,' or ' one brief, plain and uniform
grammar,' the use of which was enjoined in a special
Proclamation of ' Henry VIII, by the Grace of God,
King of England, France and Ireland, defender of
the faith, and of the Church of England, and also of
Ireland, in earth the supreme head, to all schoolmasters and teachers of grammar, within this his
realm, greeting.'  In continuation of Henry's policy

Queen Elizabeth in her Royal Injunctions in 1559, required ' that every schoolmaster and teacher shall teach the grammar set forth by King Henry VIII, of noble memory, and continued in the time of K. Edward VI.' For the carrying ' out of Henry's Proclamation and Elizabeth's Injunction, the whole ecclesiastical organisation was ready to hand. The Canons Ecclesiastical of 1571 endorsed the Injunctions and, similarly, the latest Canons (1604) confirmed (Article 79) the authorisation of Lily's *Grammar*. Before the Reformation the bishops had made visitations of all schools in their dioceses, and after the Reformation naturally the practice was of special educational significance. Thus, on the question of Lily's *Grammar*, Archbishop Cranmer in 1548 inquired in his diocese : ' Whether there be any other grammar taught in any school within this diocese than that which is set forth by the King's (Edward VI's) Majesty ? ' The same inquiry finds a place in Archbishop Parker's Visitation in 1569, in the Bishop of London's Visitation of 1571 ; in Archbishop Grindal's Visitation 1576 ; in Bishop Juxon's Visitation in 1640, and so on. The articles of inquiry in the Visitation of the Bishops, however, were much wider in scope than the question of the uniformity of use of Lily's *Grammar*. Thus in Parker's Visitation of 1567, the educational inquiry in all places of his diocese is : ' Whether your

grammar school be well ordered ? Whether the
number of children thereof be furnished ? How
many wanteth ? and by whose default ? Whether
they be diligently and godly brought up in the fear
of God, and wholesome doctrine ? whether any of
them have been received for money or reward, and
by whom ? Whether the statutes, foundations and
other ordinances touching the same grammar school,
and schoolmaster, and the scholars thereof, and any
other having doing or interest therein, are kept ?
by whom it is not observed, or by whose fault ? and
the like in all points you shall inquire and present,
of your choristers and master.'

The control thus assumed by Parker was as
absolute educationally and administratively, as ever
it could have been in pre-Reformation days. No
doubt the tradition had always been that teachers
were chosen from the clergy, and an Injunction of
Edward VI actually requires ' that all chantry priests
shall exercise themselves in teaching youths to read
and write,' but this was immediately before the act
for the dissolution of Chantries and therefore proved
nugatory, but the tradition that post-Reformation
clergymen had educational duties not dissimilar to
those of the old chantry priests may be seen in the
statement of Richard Mulcaster in 1581, in the one
passage of his *Positions* where he approximates to
the idea of universal education : ' Yet by the way

for writing and reading, so they rested there, what
if every one had them for religion's sake and their
necessary affairs.... *Every parish hath a minister,
if none else in the parish, which can help writing and
reading.*' Moreover, it would seem to have been
recognised that the post-Reformation clergyman
was actually slipping off a yoke from his neck which
the pre-Reformation chantry priest and other clergy
had more or less generally borne willingly. For
Henry VIII, Edward VI and Elizabeth taxed the
clergy to make provision for instruction and com-
pelled them to contribute towards exhibitions at
the universities and grammar schools. No doubt,
the minds of the Reformation leaders must have
been exercised severely, as to the best means of
providing a succession of clergy for parochial duties.
Accordingly the Injunctions of Queen Elizabeth
required every beneficed clergyman to give one-
thirtieth of his income to provide competent exhibitions to deserving scholars at the University and
the grammar schools, so that 'having profited in good
learning, they may be partners of their patron's cure
and charge '—thus initiating a system of curates.
In 1559 in Queen Elizabeth's Injunctions to the
Commissioners, to be given to the Chapter of Peterborough Cathedral, insistence was laid on the election
of scholars in the grammar school as apt in learning,
though ' poorest of birth,' yet such as ' are like

hereafter to be ministers in the Church.' In 1648 Matthew Poole drew up a scheme for the maintenance of 'students of choice abilities' at the university, ' principally in order to the ministry ' and collected contributions from the Presbyterians sufficient for forty scholars in each university. The responsibility financially and personally for educational progress was thus largely thrown upon the clergy. On the other hand, schoolmasters were shown great consideration in other directions. Strype in his *Annals of the Church* says that they were commonly freed from taxes and other payments and had exemptions from personal service. In 1581, when a subsidy was levied, and there were signs that schoolmasters were to be required to pay in ways not previously required, they joined in ' a humble address ' of protest to the Exchequer, the first record, Mr de Montmorency suggests, of a combination amongst schoolmasters.

The uniformity of grammar was but a slight matter compared with the ' one consent and harmony of pure and true religion ' in which Henry VIII had declared his intention to settle his people. All schoolmasters and public and private teachers were required by statute to take the oath of Supremacy. The most determined application of every resource of Church and State was brought to bear against ' recusants.' Church attendance was exacted, under rigorous penalties for absence, and every step was taken to discover and punish persistent Catholics, and above all, to prevent the children of Catholics from being trained in their parents' religion. Accordingly schools were erected by Catholics abroad. Within fifty years, at least nine such college schools were founded and pupils sent and, in cases of poverty, provided with maintenance, viz. at Douai, Rome, Valladolid, Seville, St Omer, Madrid, Louvain, Liége, Ghent—of which St Omer was founded especially for grammar, and Douai for all stages. It is 'incredible' says Thomas Fuller 'what a mass of money' was spent in the maintenance of these schools.

The strongest arm of the Church was extended in the support of the Crown against the Catholic Recusants. The bishops and Church dignitaries, we have seen, were recruited from the ranks of the 'foreign exiles,' who had lived in the atmosphere of the Genevan influence of Calvin who had brooked no leniency towards Roman Catholics, and the remembrance of Smithfield holocausts permeated the whole system of the English theologians and ecclesiastics. Even in 1638, nearly eighty years after Elizabeth's accession, in a visitation of the diocese of Norwich, the questions quoted on the next page will show the complete grip of the Church over the school organisation, and its eagle eye in the way of oversight. No wonder that the first Act of Uniformity, carried out with full penal stringency to recusants, left the grammar schools without Roman Catholic admixture. Nor is it surprising that when other forms of non-conformity arose, the same Church feared that any weakening in its absolute sway would open the floodgates to the old enemy.

The Norwich Visitation articles of Bishop Montagu asked if there were any schoolmaster in any parish who taught 'public grammar,' to write or read, or 'in private house'? 'Who are they? In whose houses do they teach? With licence or without? Do any teach in your Church or Chancel, which is to the profanation of that place? Doth any *recusant* keep a schoolmaster in his house, who cometh not to church, nor receiveth the sacrament, or is refractory to the Church orders [*i.e.* of regular attendance at services]. Doth any public schoolmaster teach the children of recusants or sectaries? Doth the schoolmaster instruct his scholars in religion, in the points of the Catechism set forth in the communion-book? Doth he orderly bring his scholars upon Sundays and holy-days, to Prayer and Sermons?' It is true inquiries were not limited to the schoolmasters. The bishops, on behalf of Church and State, asked if any 'ignorant persons' had left their trade to practise physic, or surgery; of those who practised, were they graduates licensed by their universities? (By a statute of Henry VIII dating from 1512

bishops and their vicars general had been entrusted
with the right of licensing physicians and surgeons
in their own dioceses.)   They even inquired for the
names of the midwives, and who had licensed them ?
Their rights of inquiry extended to Hospitals, Almshouses, Libraries, as well as to schools.

But there was a prior hold which the Church had
on the schoolmaster, before his practice of school-
teaching began.  In the Middle Ages, the bishops had
been required to grant licences gratis and readily to
teachers whom they might approve, but in their
control and in their control only, was placed by Canon
Law, the entrance to the teaching profession.   Immediately after Elizabeth's accession Convocation of
Canterbury re-affirmed the rule that no man should
be allowed to teach ' unless he has been approved by
the Ordinary.'

In 1581 an Elizabethan statute restrained any
person or persons, body politic or corporate, from
employing any schoolmaster, who did not ' repair
to church, and was not allowed by the Ordinary,
under a penalty of £10 a month so long as they re-
tained him ; the schoolmaster himself, presuming
to teach contrary to this act, on conviction, was to
be disabled from being a teacher,' and to be im-
prisoned without bail or mainprisé for one year.
The statute was soon put into force by preparatory
relentless inquiries from the bishops whether in any

parish there was any schoolmaster of 'suspected'
religion? Every precaution was now complete for the
removal of men of 'unsound' opinion. The ecclesiastical jurisdiction over schoolmasters was turned
into an instrument for testing loyalty to the monarch
and the Church, and for the punishment of heresy,
rather than for the promotion of education. In the
time of the Commonwealth the power of licensing
schoolmasters was not abolished, although bishops
themselves had been removed, but was exercised
by the majors-general, and sworn allegiance to the
Council of State was a necessary condition of the
schoolmaster's licence. Formerly the ecclesiastical
aspect was supreme ; in the Commonwealth the
political aspect ; in both cases the pedagogical
qualification was overshadowed.

Ecclesiastical domination over schools had led to
tyranny in the matter of these licences. Lollard
teachers had been suppressed by the Catholics.
Catholic teachers in their turn had been silenced by
the Elizabethan Church, after the Elizabethan Act
of Uniformity. Following the second Act of Uniformity, that of 1662, the ecclesiastically dominant
section of Protestantism treated the nonconformist
sections with the same persistent refusal of acknow-
ledgment that the united Protestantism of England
had meted out to Catholic teachers, in Elizabeth's
reign and onwards. Driven out from the Church,

teaching was one of the few pursuits that the expelled dissenting ministers could follow, and the refusal to allow them to teach was severe persecution. From 1662 onwards, the Nonconformist teachers ran considerable risks of prohibition and penalties, but the curious fact is that, as already stated, by the Common Law, there was the presumed citizen's right to teach school, as we have seen in the decision on the Gloucester School case. The Dissenting teachers eventually won their freedom not only as the result of the national recognition of their civil rights but also it must be remembered by the excellence of the teaching of some of their academies and private schools, to which adherents of the Church were often glad of the privilege of sending their sons. Just as France impoverished herself by the tyranny which caused the flight of the Huguenots, so 18th century education in many of the English grammar schools was almost stagnant for the lack of progressive intellects, precisely the type of men whom the Church mistakenly had excluded from the nation's schools. It was only in 1779 that dissenters became entitled by statute law to teach school at all, and they were then *expressly excluded from teaching in schools of royal foundation, or any other endowed school,* except in a school founded since 1689 for the use and benefit of Protestant dissenters. A similar statute with similar restrictions in 1790–1, gave teaching freedom to Roman Catholics, on taking an Oath of Allegiance. Apparently it was in 1846 that the sanction of punishment (imposed by the Act of Uniformity) was repealed with respect to those who taught in schools without the bishop's licence. And it was as late as 1869 that an Act required that the Endowed Schools Commissioners were to provide in every scheme for the abolition of the necessity of having the Ordinary's licence.

## CHAPTER VII

### THE CHURCH AND THE GRAMMAR SCHOOLS: RELIGIOUS OBSERVANCES AND INSTRUCTION

Not only was the outward organisation and supervision of the grammar schools ecclesiastical, but the internal atmosphere of the schools throughout the Middle Ages had been predominantly religious. The schools were a constituent part of the organisation of Collegiate Churches and of Chantries. They were, in early times, often held inside the Church, and always in its precincts, and took part in the recognised religious observances which formed the very centre of the day's life. "It is only when we notice how the Collegiate Church provided for boys in the school, the college for the same boys as men in their prime, and the hospital for the old age of those who needed it, that we see how the

Church kept in view the whole man in one institution
at all points where it was necessary to rely upon the
help of others, and the one persistent bond of union
consisted in joining together in the constant religious
services which dominated institutional life. This
aspect of medieval life in the school will be made
clear by citing the Statute of Eton College, bearing
on this subject (1440) : ' The Provost, the Fellows,
the Chaplains, the Clerks, the Scholars [*i.e.* the boys
elected on the foundation of the grammar school
of the College], and the Choristers shall on rising
say a specified antiphon, versicle, and prayer, and,
in the course of the day, a psalm, with certain ad-
juncts. Matins of the Blessed Virgin shall be said
by the Choristers in Church, and by the Scholars
in the dormitories while making their beds *before
five o'clock in the morning.* Certain other prayers
shall be said by the Usher and Scholars in School,
and, on the ringing of a bell, Scholars and Choristers
shall alike repair to the Church, to be present at the
elevation of the Host. After High Mass, about nine
o'clock, those present shall say prayers for the souls
of King Henry the Fifth and Queen Katharine,
during the life of the Founder, and afterwards for
the Founder's soul instead. Before leaving School
in the afternoon, the Scholars shall sing an antiphon
of the Blessed Virgin with certain specified versicles
and prayers, and later they shall say the Vespers of

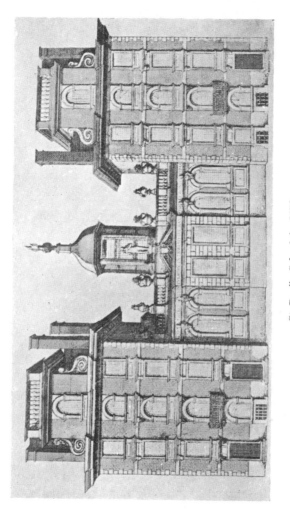

St Paul's School in 1670

NOTE.—The building in which John Milton was a school-boy was St Paul's School, as originally founded by Dean Colet. Of this there is no known illustration extant, that given above is that of the second building in 1670, the original building having been destroyed in the Great Fire of London in 1666. Strype, however, in his edition of Stowe's *London*, states that the second building was 'much after the same manner and proportion as it was before.'

the Blessed Virgin according to the ordinal of Sarum.
The Choristers shall say the Vespers and Compline
of the Blessed Virgin in the Church before the Vespers of the day.   Towards evening they shall say
the Lord's Prayer, kneeling before the great crucifix
in the Church, and sing an antiphon before the image
of the Blessed Virgin.   Further prayers shall be said
by the Fellows, the Chaplains, the Clerks, the poor
young men, the Scholars, and the Choristers, on
retiring to bed.'   In addition, the canonical hours
were to be said in the Church daily, ' according to
the use of Sarum,' beginning with Matins about five
o'clock in the morning.   The grammar school boys
were required to attend these services on the great
festivals and on certain other specified days.   The
atmosphere, therefore, was distinctly cloistral.   Dean
Colet's article on Religious Observance in his Statutes (1518) for St Paul's School, was a very considerable modification of the Eton requirement.   In
providing for a Chaplain, Colet assigns to him the
singing of mass in the Chapel of the school, where he
is to pray for the children to prosper ' in good life
and in good literature.'   At this mass whenever the
bell in the school ' shall knoll to sacring, then all the
children in the school kneeling in their seats shall
with lift-up hands, pray in the time of sacring.
After the sacring when the bell knolleth again,
they shall sit down again to their learning.'   The

chaplain was to give his time entirely to the school, in which besides singing mass, he was to teach the children the Catechism, the Articles of the faith and the Ten Commandments, in English. Colet thus combined in his Statutes the obligation on the school of providing for religious observances and for religious instruction. This direction was continued at the Reformation. The Statutes of schools after the Reformation, amid all their varieties of language, agreed substantially in three of their articles, viz. :

1. Prayers and religious observance in the grammar schools.
2. Religious instruction in the Catechism and the content of the Christian faith.
3. Attendance in a body, of the school-boys at Church, at any rate on Sundays.

The Statutes of Kirkby Stephen (Westmorland) Grammar School, 1566, put this condition of daily prayers graphically. ' I will that every morning and evening which are days for learning of scholars and keeping of school, the scholars by two and two and the schoolmaster, shall go from the schoolhouse into the Parish Church, and then devoutly upon their knees, before they do enter the choir, say some devout prayer, and after the same they shall repair together into the chapel choir, where I have made and set up a tomb, and there sing together one of the

psalms [from a list given], such as the schoolmaster
shall appoint.' Here we see a transitional stage
from the old chantry instituted for saying mass for
the soul of the founder, to the use of psalms in the
Parish Church, and a procession of the school daily
to sing them before the founder's tomb. The next
stage was to say specified prayers in the school itself,
as prescribed at East Retford Grammar School in
1552. At Sandwich Grammar School in 1580 we
get a typical Statute, in accordance with the pious
wording of everyday life after the return of the exiles.
' Acknowledging God to be the only author of all
knowledge and virtue, I ordain that the master and
usher of this my school, or one of them at least,
with their scholars at half-hour before seven of the
clock do, firstly devoutly kneeling on their knees,
pray to Almighty God, according to the form prescribed, on every school day.' The Harrow rules
of 1580 allow the prayers ' to be conceived by the
master ' and to be said by ' one whom he shall
appoint.'

Actual religious instruction was severely enjoined.
It was thought to be a matter of life and death, liter-
ally, after the experiences of Queen Mary's reign,
when nearly three hundred Protestants had been
burnt to death for their refusal to recant, that all
persons should be trained to adopt the religious
views of Elizabeth's government, which stood for

the impossibility of ever allowing Roman Catholics
to regain their old domination, and moreover that
all children should be brought up to give a reason
for the faith that was in them. The Elizabethan
fathers and mothers with their rigour of family
prayers, and readiness of mind and soul for long
services and sermons, would have insisted on school
religious exercises, even if the ecclesiastical and civil
authorities had not just as determinedly prescribed
them. All were agreed in this matter. The foreign
co-religionists, the Huguenots, were as concentrated
on religious instruction in their families ; the
mothers even training children to hardiness like the
old Spartans, to endure the agony of physical suffer-
ing, so as to be prepared for martyrdom, if necessary.
We must not, therefore, regard Queen Elizabeth's
Injunctions, and the bishops' inquiries, in their Visitations as malicious. Everyone agreed that it was a
national duty, and indeed one of the most pressing
of all national duties, that children should be trained
in the grounds of their faith in the school, equally
as in their homes. The returned exiles were not
only the dignitaries of the Church, they were the
national leaders, experienced, competent, trusted,
and in the later days, when the Counter-Reformation
of the Catholics produced keener-witted, better
trained theological disputants than Europe had
ever known, the national safety was felt to depend

not only on the wise statesmanship of Burleigh and his colleagues, but also upon the ecclesiastical and religious first line of defence in scriptural, historical and classical knowledge circulating from the universities and the schools, under the leadership of Archbishops like Grindal and Whitgift, and that capable 'consultant-educationist' in the background, Alexander Nowell, Dean of St Paul's.

It is not definitely known who wrote the short Catechism in the Book of Common Prayer—'that good unperplexed Catechism' as it is called by Izaak Walton, who did not hesitate to ascribe the authorship to the 'very learned' Nowell. The other name suggested for its authorship was John Ponet or Poynet, Bishop of Winchester in 1551, a strong reformer, also a religious refugee from Mary's persecution, who died in exile at Strassburg in 1556. Whether Nowell wrote the short Catechism mentioned or not, it is certain that he wrote the Catechisms which were semi-officially authorised for use in the grammar schools. The Prayer-book Catechism (whoever wrote it) was especially to be used in fulfilment of the Injunction of Queen Elizabeth in 1559. 'Every parson, vicar and curate shall upon every holy day and every second Sunday in the year hear and instruct the youth of the parish, for half an hour at the least before evening prayer, in the ten commandments, the Articles of the Belief and diligently examine them, and teach the Catechism set forth in the book of Public Prayer.'

Nowell published in 1570, his Catechism in two forms of very different length, known as his Longer and Shorter Catechism. The abridged form of the Longer Catechism was published as the Middle Catechism in Latin in the same year, and afterwards translated into Greek. It was the Short Catechism issued in Latin as well as in English (also translated into Greek) which became the authorised Short Catechism, for it appears to be the one sanctioned by the Canons of 1571 and confirmed by those of 1604. Though Nowell's Catechism would seem to be the most frequently used text-book, there was an enormous variety of catechetical text-books in Queen Elizabeth's reign, as well as of books of religious instruction in Calvinistic principles. Moreover, in spite of the great reputation of Nowell's Catechism, we find at Harrow the choice is given to the master between Calvin's or Nowell's Catechism, ' or some such other book at his discretion.' At Chigwell Grammar School the founder (1629) ordered that the scholars were to be prepared in the Principles of the Christian Religion by the schoolmaster for public instruction, by way of catechising, from the Vicar in the Church, which ' *I more desire than the seasoning them with learning.*'

Finally, presence of the boys of the grammar

schools with their masters was required on Sundays
and holy-days at Church, and searching examination
of the knowledge acquired from the sermon was to be
made by the schoolmaster on the Monday in school.
It has been suggested, with much likelihood, that
the beginning of taking notes in short-hand arose
from the desire to retain for after-study the main
portions of discourses which afforded satisfaction to
the hearers in founding and establishing ' principles '
of Christian teaching.    Even the text-books for
learning Latin emphasised the religious side of life.
No book of ' Colloquies ' (the favourite method of
teaching Latin-speaking) was so popular for young
boys as that of Corderius, the schoolmaster of
Calvin.    Dialogues are there given between little
boys discussing the sermon, confessing that they
deserved stripes if they had not succeeded in com-
mitting at least part of it to memory.    They
pray in school four or five times openly.    They
pray at meals, on going to bed, on rising, but the
master admonishes them also to go apart at times for
secret prayer, even if it is difficult to acquire the
habit.    They learn scripture texts to establish their
religious opinions, and to induce the practice of right
actions.    When they take walks with a master, he
practises each boy in ' capping ' sentences from the
New Testament.    In the summer, they take a psalm-
book with them to sing somewhere in the shade ' so

that their walk may be the more pleasant.' And, before each action in daily life they are taught to say ' God willing.' God is King and Ruler in every event of life, great and small, and His Will is to be found in the Scriptures, which are His Word.

Thus the medieval cloistral institutional life, as it changed to the life of Elizabethan times, involved less of ceremonial and symbolical and picturesque services for boys, but just as constant a recognition of religion, in the family life at home, in the school, in the Church. The national life was wrapt up in its political and social aspects, and, with the Puritans, depended upon the maintenance of a religious scheme of life that developed the individual's sense of responsibility before God, inspiring a sense of awe, of prostrate humility in the worship of Him, but of fear of Him alone. Thus the stern, strong, irresistible features of Puritanic individualism became ingrained deeper and deeper by means of the very educational organisation developed by preceding generations, with the aim of corporate action calculated to suppress all individuality.

# CHAPTER VIII

## THE GRAMMAR SCHOOL CURRICULUM

Though the grammar schools were controlled
externally by ecclesiastical authority (placed at the
service of the King as Head of the Church), and
internally, by the religious principles and doctrines
with which the minds of parents and schoolmasters
of the Elizabethan and Stuart periods were saturated,
it must not be supposed that the original purpose of
the grammar schools to teach Latin grammar was
overlooked in the presence of the absorbing issues
of religious teaching. Naturally, to some extent,
and in some directions, the classical aims were
modified. Thus, Laurence Humphrey, the returned
exile, President of Magdalen College, the Oxford
college with specially puritanic tendencies, made a
determined protest against the reading of Ovid and
other authors ' in whom they study strange tongues
to the decay of godliness.' Humphrey's suggested
Latin course, which may be taken as that of a representative Puritan of the learned type in Elizabeth's
reign included : precepts of rules of grammar in an
abridged form ; Cicero's *Epistles*, and those *Colloquies* of Erasmus and of Castellion [a French edu-
cationist in Geneva in the time of Calvin who turned

the chief Scriptural stories into dialogue form for the teaching of Latin]. The latter was chosen ' timely to sow the seeds of godliness and virtue in their tender hearts.' Then followed Terence, ' but with riper years and judgment. If any filth be intermeddled let the teacher use sounder authors as treacle [*i.e.* an antidote] to expel it. Nor would I yield Terence this room but for I saw Cicero so much esteem him, who took not the least part of eloquence of him, as Chrysostom of Aristophanes the eloquence of the Attic tongue, a poet nevertheless both nipping in taunts and wanton in tales....Not little helpeth it, even at first, to learn them Greek and Hebrew, *preposterously do all Universities, schools and teachers that contrary it.* For about the bush run they to arts, who understand not the original tongues.' Humphrey's book (*The Nobles*) was first published in Latin (as *Optimates*) in 1560. Appropriately to its Swiss cast of thought, it was published at Basle. It is worth noting that it is one of the books printed in the transition stage of English, which was not as yet employed by scholars writing to scholars in England. It was therefore first written in Latin, and translated into English, as an afterthought, for a public of readers hitherto unreached. This public was chiefly those newly taught to read for the purpose of religious instruction and edification.

This recoil against the impurity to be found in

classical writings developed into such intensity of
antagonism that about 1630 we find John Amos
Comenius wishing Latin to be learned, by studying
those authors alone who, writing in the Latin
language, included only the subject-matter of useful
knowledge in the arts and sciences.

One marked distinction of Protestantism from
Catholicism was that the liturgy of the former ap-
peared in the vernacular, whilst Catholic services
always had been conducted in the Latin language.
This difference tended to take away the stronghold of
Latin, in the minds of convinced Protestants, and certainly altered teaching methods.  Thus, apparently,
in pre-Reformation times, Latin grammar was the
*first* subject of learning in the grammar school.
Richard Mulcaster in 1581, suggested a revision of
this position.  'While our religion,' says he, ' was
restrained to the Latin, it was either the onely, or
the oneliest principle in learning, to learn to read
Latin : as most appropriate to that effect, which
the Church then esteemed on most.  But now, now
that we are returned home to our English A B C,
as most natural to our soil, and most proper to our
faith, we are to be directed by nature and property
[*i.e.* suitability] to read that first, which we speak
first.'  It is, however, possible with the lack of
any fixed standard of English in pre-Reformation
times that a good Latin grammar in Latin gave a

better start for the pupil, whilst after the great
literary achievements in the vernacular of the Elizabethan age, Mulcaster's plea for teaching in the
vernacular became sound, even from the point of
view of a more thorough acquisition of the early
stages of Latin.

On the other hand, the Protestant demand for
the reading of the Bible, logically enough, as we see
in Humphrey, led to the manifest requirement of the
study of the 'holy' languages, Greek, Hebrew and
Latin, associated with the earliest MSS. of the Bible.
Moreover, when the great controversies arose between
Protestant and Catholic theologians, Latin and Greek
became still more urgent studies, to be prepared for
betimes in the grammar schools, because appeals to
patristic literature could only be sustained by
developed power in rendering the original Latin or
Greek into English.

And, again, the Elizabethan leaders of English
theology, in the first instance so often religious exiles
keenly interested in the application of their foreign
educational experiences, on their return to England,
engaged in extensive and continued correspondence
with foreign leaders of the highest erudition. This
continued intercourse brought English educators and
schoolmasters into touch with continental standards,
and with the main current of European thought and
practice. This could be illustrated by many examples

of the foreign text-books (in Latin) in use in English schools, of which we have already noted Calvin's Catechism and the *Colloquies* of the Genevan Corderius and Castellion. Nor must it be forgotten that, after St Bartholomew's Massacre, Huguenot refugees received a welcome in England. Foreign schoolmasters came over, for example, Adrian Saravia, who was headmaster, for a time, of Southampton Grammar School. More important still in setting a high standard of classical attainments, and in raising upwards the standard of expectation from the grammar school classical training, was the practice of the Church of conferring benefices in English Cathedrals upon distinguished foreign scholars. It will be remembered that in pre-Reformation days, the great Erasmus had been thus recognised by the bestowal on him by Archbishop Warham of the living of Aldington in Kent, although Erasmus was ignorant of the English language and could not make a pretence of discharging parochial duties. Isaac Casaubon, one of the greatest classical scholars of any age, was a Prebendary of Canterbury and his son, Meric Casaubon, later carried on the tradition of erudition, as a prebendary of the same Cathedral. Gerard John Vossius, a classical scholar of European reputation, after being a professor at Leyden, in its great days of academic leadership, was invited to England, and made a Canon of Canterbury. His son, too, was afterwards brought to England and appointed Canon of Windsor, and when he died it was said he left behind him ' the best private library in the world.' Such men as the Casaubons and the Vossiuses stimulated English scholarship in a high degree. Great scholarly works were produced in the period immediately succeeding Elizabeth, such as the text of St Chrysostom by Savile ; the translation of the Bible by a large body of Greek and Hebrew scholars, and later, the Polyglot Bible of Brian Walton. Besides Biblical scholarship, there was great study in the early fathers and schoolmen, in disputational and theological learning, as well as in the Latin, Greek and Hebrew and Oriental languages.

It was in this period, too, that works abounding in incidental, illustrative learning were welcomed by readers, such as the *Anatomy of Melancholy* of Robert Burton ; the *Religio Medici* of Sir Thomas Browne ; the *Histrio-Mastix* of William Prynne. The highest scholarship, bringing on England the notice of every European centre of learning, was shown in Ussher, Gataker, and Selden. The learning of the preachers, Sandys, Jewel, Hooker, the ' silver tongued Henry Smith,' Launcelot Andrewes, Donne, on to Jeremy Taylor was only possible in an age in which not only great classicists were the admired leaders of learning, but also indirectly bears witness to a sound appreciation by the readers of classical and patristic allusion, such as could only be developed from a persistent and concentrated application to 'grammar' studies in the old sense of the term.

As to the actual subjects of the curriculum of the grammar schools, there is abundance of material for tracing both the content and the methods of teaching. In the first place, there are the School Statutes and Orders; in the second, a book on the subject by John Brinsley in 1612, and another book by Charles Hoole in 1660—just over a century after the accession of Queen Elizabeth, and thirdly, incidental references by schoolmasters, scholars, and observers.

John Brinsley's book is called *Ludus Literarius, or the Grammar School* (first edition 1612, second 1627). He describes methods of procedure from 'the first entrance into learning to the highest perfection required in the Grammar Schools.' Though he claims that all he writes is 'only according to our common grammar and ordinary classical authors,' yet his work is offered 'for the perpetual benefit of Church and Commonwealth.' The late R. H. Quick wrote in his copy of this work, 'no other book throws such light on the teaching in English schools at the beginning of the sixteen hundreds.' We may note from the title of his book, Brinsley is of Roger Ascham's opinion that the grammar school should be 'indeed, as it is called by name, "the house of play."'

This did not seem inconsistent to Brinsley, stern
Puritan as he was, and though, it should be stated,
he was the translator into English (for the purpose
of re-translation by boys into Latin) of Corderius's
*Colloquies*, which includes the dialogues described
on p. 91, and scores of passages of similar pietistic
import. It must be confessed, too, that Charles
Hoole is also intent on the cultivation of the religious
tone and doctrine as the atmosphere of every rightly
regulated grammar school. As Hoole incorporates
most of the essential features of Brinsley's description of the inner work of the grammar schools, and
brings it up to date, there is no book which contains
so thorough an account as his of the curricula of
the best grammar schools, about the middle of the
17th century, when they were at their best, taken
as a whole, the country through. Although Hoole
published his *New Discovery of the Old Art of Teaching
School*, as he calls it, in 1660, it is based on experience
which went back to before the great Civil War, and
he distinctly states that he owes much to his own
schoolmaster, Robert Doughty, headmaster of Wakefield Grammar School, and to his predecessor in the
headmastership of Rotherham Grammar School,
Mr Bonner. After he left Rotherham Hoole under-
took the management of a private grammar school,
during some years of his life in Aldersgate Street,
and afterwards in Lothbury, and we are told by

Anthony à Wood, that he instructed youths 'to a miracle.'

In the preparatory or 'petty' school, Hoole requires that the Alphabet should be taught by means of play. Reading requires a capable teacher. Not only books of religion and manners are to be used but also delightful books of English history, Herbert's *Poems* and Quarles' *Emblems*. This is apparently the first instance of the recommendation of English literature for school teaching. Erasmus's *de Moribus* and Hawkins' *Youth's Behaviour* should be taught for 'manners.' The Primer, the Psalter, the Bible are to be used for teaching, spelling and reading. Writing and casting accounts are to be taught. The Lord's Prayer, the Creed, the Ten Commandments and the Catechism are to be known by all. Like Matthew Arnold later, Hoole would have elementary Latin learned even by those whose education did not proceed beyond the elementary stage. For, Hoole thinks a little Latin is useful 'in the understanding of *English* authors.'

Coming to the grammar school proper, the curriculum should be, following closely Hoole's account of the syllabus (form by form):

Form I. This form to be occupied for a year in preparing the pupils for the Latin tongue by teaching them the perfect use of the accidence, helping them to a vocabulary of words, and showing

how to vary them.   The *Introduction* to the Latin
Grammar, and *Sententiae pueriles,* and a little
*Vocabulary* are to be used as text-books.   In this
form Hoole recommends the use of Comenius's *Orbis
Pictus* (a pictorial Latin primer), so as to encourage
the training of observation.   The principles of
Christianity were to be taught on Saturdays.

With regard to the work of Form I, it should be
stated that Statutes of some grammar schools lay
down that, as a condition for admission, boys should
be well grounded in accidence, know the concords, and
be competent in reading and writing.   With regard to
the boys who came to grammar schools not having
passed through a preparatory or petty school, Hoole
requires that either the boy can write or that he be
sent concurrently to a writing school, an institution
in the largest towns, conducted by a private schoolmaster, for fees, in which writing and arithmetic
were taught.   In country grammar schools, a
scrivener went from place to place, staying a few
weeks at a time to try to establish the writing of the
boys, and then left the teachers to keep it in practice,
but teaching writing was no part of the work of a
free grammar school, and if taught, was paid for as
an extra.

Form II is to be exercised in :
1.   Repeating the accidence.
2.   The parts of nouns and verbs.

3. Learning a larger vocabulary.

4. Learning *Qui mihi* [*i.e.* Lily's version of the life and manners of a grammar school boy], and afterwards Cato twice a week, and *Pueriles Confabulatiunculae* twice a week.

5. Translating a verse out of English into Latin every evening at home.

' Thus they may be made to know the genders of nouns, preter-perfect tenses and supine of verbs, and be initiated to speak and write true Latin in the compass of a second year.'

In this form children were to have little paper books (as indeed Roger Ascham had previously suggested in 1570) wherein they were to enter choice phrases from classical authors, and so avoid Anglicisms.

Form III. To be employed about three-quarters of a year :

1. In reading four or six verses out of the Latin Testament every morning.

2. In repeating syntaxes and accidence.

3. In Aesop's *Fables*.

4. In Comenius's *Janua Linguarum*.

5. In Baptista Mantuan's *Eclogues* and Helvicus's *Colloquies*.

6. In the Assembly's Latin Catechism—on Saturdays.

7. In translating every night two verses out

of the Proverbs into Latin—and two out of the Latin Testament into English.

One quarter of the year should be spent chiefly in getting Figura (*i.e.* the ' figures ' of rhetoric) and Prosody. This third year will be ' well bestowed in teaching children of between nine and ten years of age the whole grammar and the right use of it.'

As to Aesop's *Fables* (of which it will be remembered John Locke, later, made an interlinear translation into English of the Latin text), Hoole declares that it is a book of great antiquity and ' of more solid learning than most men think.' For it teaches morality by its epilogues, ' which do insinuate themselves into every man's mind.' In Form III each pupil keeps a paper book *in quarto* in which to enter rules and exceptions, and to make collections of ' pregnant examples ' from Latin authors.

At this stage, the pupil passes from the care of the usher, or under-master, to that of the master, who will test closely the pupil in his exact knowledge of grammar, *i.e.* in Lily's grammar before he receives him.

Form IV. Scholars of this form are required :

1. Every morning to read six or ten verses out of the Latin Testament into English, that then they may become well acquainted with the matter and words of ' that most holy book '; and after they

are entered in Greek to proceed with the Greek
Testament in like manner.

2.  To say over again, once a quarter, the
whole Latin grammar.  Each pupil is to have a
paper book of two quires in quarto, into which,
under right heads, he is to note all niceties of grammar,  with which he meets.  The older critical
grammarians are to be consulted and perused.  Every
school should have its library, in which should be
placed all the best grammars.  Boys should then be
encouraged to read them and to cite what they find
striking in them, and place it under its proper head,
in the paper book.

3.  Rhetoric, three mornings a week.  Text-
books :  *Elementa Rhetorices*, that lately printed by
William  Dugard,  of  Merchant  Taylors'  School,
together with that by Talaeus and that of Charles
Butler.  They are to make a synopsis of Dugard's
text-book, and to enter into a commonplace book
' whatever they like ' from other writers on Rhetoric.

4.  When they have passed through a course
in Rhetoric, the time given to it should be transferred
to Greek grammar.  ' And because,' says Hoole,
' in learning this language as well as the Latin, we
are to proceed by one rule which is most common and
certain ; I prefer Camden's *Greek Grammar*, though
perhaps it is not so facile or so complete as some
latelier printed, especially those that are set out by

my worthy friends, Mr Busby of Westminster and Mr Dugard of Merchant Taylors'.'

Westminster School was famous for its study of Greek. In 1575 Edward Grant, headmaster, wrote the first Greek Grammar in English. This was adopted in 1597 by William Camden, whose *Greek Grammar* became to Greek what Lily's was to Latin, in the grammar schools of the country, and similarly was taken over as the Eton Greek Grammar, but at Westminster itself it was superseded by Dr Busby's *Greek Grammar*. The fine Greek printer at Cambridge, Roger Daniel, paid a unique tribute to the Greek scholarship of Westminster School, when he dedicated the first Greek text in England of the Septuagint version of the Old Testament to 'the boys' in Westminster School.

The first quarter of a year should be taken up with going over Greek letters, accents, and parts of speech, articles, declensions, conjugations, adverbs, conjunctions and prepositions, and exercises in writing (including accents). The next half-year the whole grammar is covered. Every morning the pupils are to use their Greek Testaments after prayers, beginning with the Gospel of St John.

'If you would have them learn to speak Greek let them make use of Posselius's *Dialogues*, or Mr Shirley's *Introductorium* in English, Latin and Greek.'

5. Terence, to be read four mornings a week, taking about half a page at a time till the pupils begin to relish him. The most significant words and phrases are to be culled out, and entered into a paper book.

6. The *Janua Latinae Linguae* of J. A. Comenius, to strengthen vocabulary.

7. Cicero's *Epistolae* or the *Epistolae* of Textor. Double translation should be employed. This should lead to the writing of epistles. Two epistles to be written every week, one in answer to the other.

8. For a half-year, two afternoons a week, Ovid's *de Tristibus*, six or eight verses at a lesson to be repeated by memory. English verses to be written, with models in George Herbert's and Quarles' poems. In the second half-year, Ovid's *Metamorphoses* are prescribed. Pupils may also translate four passages into Latin every night out of *Wit's Commonwealth* and then translate them into Greek. On Saturdays : The Assembly's Catechism.

Form V.

1. Every day twelve verses at least in the Greek Testament.

2. Repeat the Latin and Greek grammars and the *Elementa Rhetorices*.

3. Let them pronounce orations out of Livy, etc., three days a week.

4. Read Isocrates, for three-quarters of the year, and in the fourth, Theognis.

5. Read Justin's *History*, Caesar's *Commentaries*, Lucius Florus, intermixing some of Erasmus's *Colloquies*.

6. The *Janua Linguarum Graeca* for vocabulary.

7. Virgil.

8. Aesop's *Fables* (in Greek), Aelian's *Histories*, Epictetus, or Farnaby's *Epigrammata*.

9. The making of Themes.

10. Writing verses in Latin.

11. Nowell's *Catechism*, or the Palatinate Catechism, to be learned.

For the making of Latin Themes, pupils must first be taught how to collect the subject-matter, and where to help themselves with words and phrases, how to dispose the parts, and what *formulae* they are to use in passing from one part to another. They will thus have to learn how to find and use material, as for instance, in the following ways :

Short histories from Plutarch, Valerius Maximus, Justin, Caesar, Florus, Livy, Pliny, *Medulla Historiae*, Aelianus. Apologues and fables out of Aesop, Phaedrus, Ovid, Natalis Comes. Adages from Erasmus, Drax, etc. Hieroglyphics from Pierius and Caussinus. Emblems and symbols, to be collected from Alciat, Beza, Reusner, etc. Ancient laws and customs are to be gathered from Plutarch, etc. Witty sentences from *Golden Grove, Moral Philosophy, Sphinx Philosophica, Wit's Commonwealth*, Tully's sentences, *Demosthenis Sententiae*, etc. Rhetorical exornations out of Vossius, Farnaby, Butler, etc. Topical places out of Caussinus, Tesmarus, *Orator extemporaneus*, etc. Descriptions of things natural and artificial out of *Orbis Pictus*, Caussinus, Pliny, etc.

Form VI. Their constant employment is :

1. To read twelve verses out of the Greek Testament every morning.

2. To repeat Latin and Greek grammar and *Elementa Rhetorices*.

3. To learn Hebrew, three days a week. Text-book : Buxtorf's Grammar.

4. To read Hesiod, Homer, Pindar, and Lycophron.

5. To read Xenophon, Sophocles, Euripides, and Aristophanes.

6. Study the *Breviarium Graecae Linguae* of Ant. de Laubegeois twice a week.

7. Read Horace, Juvenal, Persius, Lucan, Seneca's *Tragedies*, Martial and Plautus.

8. Lucian's *Select Dialogues* and Pontanus' *Progymnasmata Latinitatis*.

9. Cicero's *Orations*, Pliny's *Panegyrics*, Quintilian's *Declamationes*, Godwin's *Antiquities* to be read at leisure times.

10.  Their exercises for oratory should be to
make themes, orations, and declamations, in Latin,
Greek and Hebrew, and for poetry to make verses
upon such themes as are appointed every week.

11.  To exercise themselves in making ana-
grams, epigrams, epitaphs, epithalamia, eclogues,
and acrostics, in English, Latin, Greek, Hebrew.

12.  The Catechisms to be used are Nowell
and Birket (Berchet) in Greek, and the Church
Catechism in Hebrew.

Hoole offers a 'Note of School Authors' for the
school library running to between 250 and 300 books
including classical authors, grammars, vocabularies,
dictionaries, fables, dialogues, rhetoric, oratory,
letters, phrases, anthologies, etc., and leading works
of reference on the professional subjects of the
theologian, physician and lawyer.  The reading of the
authors can only mean selections of their works, but
the disciplinary aspect of the theme-writing and orations, together with the wisdom manifested in some
of the teaching methods, shows that the work contemplated and attempted in grammar schools was
severe and exacting, and required the exercise of a
selective judgment in writing at every stage.

The wide training thus sketched, even if only
partially accomplished in many cases, discloses in
the grammar schools a conscious aim and aspira-
tion, and explains how it was that to some extent,

at least, Englishmen took an intelligent interest in the learned literature produced by Robert Burton, Sir Thomas Browne, John Selden,—and especially by John Milton,—in a degree, one is obliged to think, relatively to the population, surpassing the interest taken by our own generation in learned works.

## CHAPTER IX

### THE OLD GRAMMAR SCHOOL INTERNAL LIFE

Adaptation to local surroundings was character-istic of the provincial grammar schools, in spite of all attempts of the central authorities and ecclesias-tical supervisors to secure uniformity in certain directions. The Statutes of the individual schools therefore show the greatest variety of intention and aim. The new part taken by laymen in the foundation of schools in the 15th century naturally led to diver-sity of educational ideas in the Statutes, and even in pre-Reformation times, laymen had charge of grammar schools. The differentiation of the pro-fession of teaching from that of the clergy, has proceeded slowly, yet in the Orders of St Albans Grammar School, devised by Sir Nicholas Bacon in 1570, it was declared 'that the schoolmaster shall have *no other service or charge* that might withdraw

him from his duty as schoolmaster,' and in 1574 ' the
Wardens and four Assistants of the Town and Parish
of Sevenoaks,' in whom was vested the government
of the Free Grammar School of Queen Elizabeth at
Sevenoaks, in Kent, by their Statutes required themselves and their successors to choose for their master
' one honest and mete man, sufficiently learned and
expert in grammar, *not being in Holy Orders*, to
teach grammar in the school.' It is true, on the
other hand, some of the school Statutes required
that a ' priest ' should be appointed. But it is clear
that the transition stage towards teaching becoming
a sufficient profession of itself had set in.

In pre-Reformation times, ' the inhabitants ' of
various townships had founded chantries, for the
purpose of providing instruction in grammar and
this movement was continued after the Reformation.
And in post-Reformation times towns were deeply
interested in those young men who had gone away
and made their fortunes, and then returned to found
a school in their birthplace. Grammar schools re-
vealed themselves as the institutions which made
possible ecclesiastical, commercial, social advance-
ment for the individual. Some schools were associated with local interests still more closely. For
instance the income of Manchester Grammar School
was provided from the profits of corn mills, in which
the inhabitants had their corn ground, it is stated,

Grantham Grammar School, founded 1528; refounded 1553

(*Where [Sir] Isaac Newton was a pupil*)

till 1759. St Albans Grammar School was endowed by a 'wine Charter' obtained for it by Sir Nicholas Bacon. One of the guiding principles of the re-foundation of grammar schools adopted by Edward VI, and continued by Queen Elizabeth, was to place the school (sometimes even when there was a private founder) under the control or direction of the Town Corporation. Thus, to take examples, in the single county of Lincolnshire, the Free Grammar School at Great Grimsby was founded by letters patent in the first year of Edward VI, 1547, and the management fell to the Corporation, as Trustees. In 1552, Louth Grammar School, also 'founded' by letters patent of King Edward VI, prescribed that the ' said town of Louth be corporate of one Warden of the town of Louth and Free School in the same, and of six Assistants, inhabiting in the said town for ever.' In 1553, the Free Grammar School at Grantham (founded originally by Richard Fox, Bishop of Winchester, and native of near Grantham) was augmented by Edward VI, who, upon the petition of the Aldermen and Burgesses, by letters patent granted that there should be *one* grammar school in the said town, and placed with the Aldermen and Burgesses the appointment of the master; and with the advice of the Bishop of the diocese, or during the vacancy of the see, with the advice of the master of St John's College in Cambridge from time to time, to make Statutes and Ordinances.  In 1554, Queen Mary founded and endowed Boston Grammar School and in 1567 the Mayor and Burgesses of the town erected a new school house, and the management, either then or originally, was placed in the hands of the Mayor and Burgesses.  In Lincoln, there were two grammar schools, one of the Cathedral, dating probably from the 11th century, and the other under the city corporation, of long standing.  In 1583 these two ancient schools were united, and for a long time the master was appointed by the Dean and Chapter who submitted his name to the corporation.  In the last century, a differentiation of the school into upper and lower, or classical and modern sides took place, the Dean and Chapter continuing the management of the upper and the corporation taking charge of the lower school, and although the classes were held in the same building for some time, the two schools were substantially separate.

In the same way it might be shown in other counties of England that the grammar schools became associated with the town authorities, and that municipal interest was thus aroused in what the inhabitants regarded as 'their' school, for the schools were open to all who satisfied the conditions of entrance, and often free of fees for 'grammar' instruction. The conditions for holding masterships and the conditions of entrance for scholars are usually laid down

in the Statutes with considerable fulness. Colet had
required for his master at St Paul's (1518) that he
should be 'a man whole in body, honest and virtuous,
and learned in good and clean Latin literature and
also in Greek, if such may be gotten'; at Oundle
(Northants.) the Wardens of the Grocers' Company
ordain that their master shall be ' whole of body, of
good report, and in degree a master of arts, mete for
his learning and *dexterity in teaching*, and of right
understanding of good and true religion set forth by
public authority, whereunto he shall move and stir
his scholars.' At Thame (1574) on election, the
master read out at Church the Statute which
eloquently and in detail explained his functions
and responsibilities; at Kirkby Stephen, 1566,
(Westmorland) he took an oath on entering his office,
in the parish church. At East Retford, 1552, the
master was ' sworn upon the Holy Bible before the
Archbishop of York or his deputy, to do his duty,'
whereupon six of the Bailiffs and Burgesses of the
Town proceeded to put the master ' in possession of
his room.'

The conditions of entrance for boys varied greatly
in their strictness, but the fact that the education was
usually ' free ' made it necessary to exercise restric-
tion in cases where the school was popular. It is
clear that the advice of Becon for the foundation of
grammar schools for ' youth of the female kind '

was not taken.  In the Harrow Rules (1590) it is
expressly stated that ' no girls shall be received to be
taught in the school,' a rule which seems to suggest
some possible danger in that direction in the absence
of direct prohibition.  At Bunbury Grammar School
in Cheshire, founded in 1594, girls were, by statute,
to be admitted, but the number was limited, and none
were to remain ' above the age of nine, nor longer
than they may learn to read English.'  The Statutes
of Harrow (1590) require the scholars to be of ' the
poorest sort,' but with the limitation, 'if they shall
be apt.'  In view of the marvellous development of
Harrow into an aristocratic ' non-local ' Public
School, it is interesting to recall the original Statute
with regard to ' non-local ' pupils.  ' And of the
*foreigners*, the master may take such stipend and
wages as he can get, except that they be of the kindred
of John Lyon the founder : so that [*i.e.* as long as]
he take pains with all indifferently as well of the
parish as foreigners, as well of poor as of rich : but
the discretion of the Governors shall be looked to that
he do.'

The entrance age was usually seven years,
though sometimes six and sometimes eight was
prescribed.  ' Six,' says Brinsley, ' is very young.'
Physical ' wholeness ' was sometimes prescribed in
accordance with Roger Ascham's claim that the
child destined for learning should be εὐφυής (*i.e.*

well endowed by nature, at any rate physically).
Even if there were no tuition fees, there was often
an ' admission ' or registration fee. The reason is
thus given by Dean Colet, viz. that the poor scholar
who is told off ' to sweep the school and keep it clean,'
may be paid by receiving the ' money of the ad-
missions.' At Alford Grammar School (1599) it was
decreed that none be admitted before ' he can read
perfectly, and write legibly,' and it was no part of the
duty of the schoolmaster to teach any of his scholars
to write. This was an ideal condition aimed at by
masters, but it was not always realised. Dean Colet
had laid down in his ' Articles of Admission ' the
condition to which close attention should be paid by
the reader desirous to understand the aims of the
grammar schools of the 16th and 17th centuries. ' If
your child,' the master is to ' rehearse ' to the parent,
' after reasonable season proved, be found here unapt
and unable to learning, then ye, warned thereof shall
take him away, that he occupy not here room in vain.'
On the other hand if the child were found apt, the
parent was to agree that he should remain in the
school ' till he have competent literature.' A similar
provision was inserted at Oundle, 1556, and in
St Albans Statutes, 1570. Alford Grammar School
Statutes, 1590, are to the same purport.

It would seem as if Mulcaster was serious when
he said : ' everyone desireth to have his children

learned.' But he is hard-hearted against the over-
flow of boys into the grammar schools. ' *Only boys
of real power* should be received, whether poor *or*
rich ; the latter by private help if the parents are
wealthy, or by public aid if poverty pray for it.'
In pre-Reformation days ' the Church was an
harbour for all men to ride in,' if they were ' lettered.'
Livings were ' infinite ' in number. ' The expelled
religion was supported by multitude, and the more
who had interest in it, the more stood for it,' but the
reformed church ' must pitch the defence of her truth
in some *paucity of choice* ' for the old church ' livings,'
so many of them, had vanished. Care must be taken
to choose the fittest kinds of ' wits ' only, for learning ;
and even with them as pupils, Mulcaster sagely warns
schoolmasters and parents against ' over-haste.'

Boys went to the university early, commonly
in their 16th year, though they sometimes went in
the time of the early Tudors at 12 years. The
numbers in the grammar schools were very various.
St Saviour's Grammar School, Southwark (1562),
was to have not more than 100 boys ; St Albans
Grammar School (1570), 120, and Blundell's School,
Tiverton, 150. But schools were sometimes very
small. For instance, Queen Elizabeth endowed a
grammar school at Penryn, in Cornwall, for a master
there to teach three boys. Bath Grammar School
was founded (1553) for the education of 10 poor boys.

Dedham Grammar School (1571), in Essex, provided
for 20 boys.  But on the other hand, Merchant
Taylors' School, London, was planned for 250 boys,
whilst at Shrewsbury the numbers at one time
reached 360 and indeed later are said to have reached
600.  It is described by William Camden as the ' best
filled school in England,' but Shrewsbury had no
greater distinction than that of numbering Sir
Philip Sidney amongst its pupils.

No feature of the old grammar schools strikes
our generation with more surprise than the hours of
school work.  The usual working hours in the
summer were from 6 till 11 o'clock in the morning
and in the afternoon from 1 o'clock till 6 o'clock (as
at Sevenoaks Grammar School).  In the winter the
general rule was from 7 till 11 o'clock in the morning
and from 1 to 5 o'clock in the afternoon.  Since the
school hours in winter required the use of artificial
light, it was the custom for boys to be required to
pay for their own candles.  Thus, by the Guildford
Grammar School Statutes, each boy was ' to pay 4d.
at the Feast of St Michael yearly, wherewith shall be
bought clean waxen candles to keep light in the school
during winter.'  Dean Colet forbade the use of
tallow candles at St Paul's and decreed that only
wax candles be used and these ' at the cost of the
boys' friends.'  At Shrewsbury the hours were, from
Lady Day to All Saints Day, 6 to 11 a.m., 12.45 to

5.30 p.m. From All Saints Day to Lady Day,
7 to 11 a.m. and 12.45 to 4.30 p.m. if daylight served.
In summer the boys were at work in school for either
9 or 10 hours, and in winter for 7 or 8 hours a day.
They had evening work also, at any rate, in some
schools. Nor were the holidays long as we should
think. At Shrewsbury 18 days were allowed at
Christmas, 12 days at Easter and 9 days at
Whitsuntide. But this was for a great boarding
school which included sons of nobles and gentry.
For the local schools, the holidays were after the
type of Alford, where it is stated in the Orders of
1590 the masters shall not 'break up the school at
any times in the year, but from the even of St Thomas
the Apostle before the Feast of the Nativity until the
next day after the Epiphany, and again from the
Tuesday before Easter-day until the Sunday next after
Easter-day, except great sickness shall enforce there-
unto,' *i.e.* the holidays were twice a year of 16 days
and 12 days respectively. 'Remedies' [*i.e.* holidays
for play] were allowed except at St Paul's where Colet
ordained that ' the children shall have no remedies.'
Dean Nowell, we remember, suggested that one a
week ' might be borne with.' His suggestion, indeed,
became the rule, later, and boys had a half-holiday
each of the 48 working weeks of the year. The
holy-days not spent in school lessons were often
mortgaged by outside work, *e.g.* writing and ' devout

and virtuous endeavours and exercises' (whatever these were) as the Statutes at Kirkby Stephen prescribe, and they might be required either in the school or in the Church. The half-holidays referred to might be granted by the master or ' at the pleasure of some honourable or worshipful person,' and the writer can remember, in his school days, how in a particular grammar school, under the government of the Town Council, the Mayor used to send át times to the school his officer, who raised, in the presence of masters and boys, his finger on which was an official ring, in token of the Mayor's desire that the school that afternoon should have a holiday.

The time, therefore, spent in work was on the whole, enormous; and this fact helps to explain the possibility of attempting the different sides of classical discipline described in the last chapter. A boy stayed, as a rule, in the grammar school six, sometimes seven, years. If he came under a really erudite scholar and capable teacher, the authors read, and the methods of training in Latin composition and style, produced a good classicist, and a man in touch with the knowledge of his age,—for the subject-matter studied in the schools, was much wider in scope than is often supposed, for the simple reason that wise schoolmasters chose, as subjects for theses, topics which could be illustrated by examples from the arts and sciences, from history and literature, chiefly from Latin writers, *modern* as well as ancient, and also from writers in the vernacular; and even from authors using modern languages. Often the classical masters were men of wide experience and knowledge. Ashton, headmaster of Shrewsbury, was accomplished as a courtier; Sir Henry Savile and Sir Henry Wotton, provosts of Eton, were men of the widest culture and travel. Richard Knolles, who wrote a *History of the Turks* in good strong English style, was headmaster of Sandwich school. A man of travels and historical study like Camden, must have been an inspiring teacher of many subjects—over and above ' mere ' Latinity. Philemon Holland, the versatile and erudite scholar, is not likely to have given a narrow training in classical studies, whilst headmaster of Coventry Grammar School. William Malim, a headmaster of Eton, had travelled to Antioch, Constantinople, Jerusalem and other Eastern cities. And later lived Thomas Farnaby, educated in a Jesuit college in Spain, a companion of Drake and Hawkins in their last voyage in 1595, and afterwards a soldier in the Netherlands, who, on his return to England became a teacher first at Martock in Somersetshire, and afterwards set up a private grammar school in Goldsmith's Rents in Cripplegate in London. Farnaby was esteemed by some the greatest classical scholar in England, and his reputation was European. He was a friend

of Ben Jonson, G. J. Vossius, and Meric Casaubon.
He built an imposing school-house, and—an innovation in grammar schools—is said to have had a separate class-room for the different forms, and kept good
ushers.  The number of pupils reached 300 and the
school attracted the sons of some of the 'highest
families in the land.  He is said to have been the first
schoolmaster in England to have made a fortune.

The Elizabethan grammar schools in their attention to Roman history were not oblivious of the
glorious past of England.  John Twyne, headmaster
of the King's School, Canterbury, and John Langley,
headmaster of St Paul's School, London, were, like
Camden of Westminster School, distinguished British
antiquaries.   John Hyrd, headmaster of Lincoln
Grammar School (1580), wrote in Latin verse a
*Historia Anglicana*, and Christopher Ocland of
Southwark School, also in 1580, wrote the *Anglorum
Praelia*, singing the praises of Creçy and Agincourt,
just before the time of the Spanish Armada.
Ocland's book received the remarkable honour of
being the subject of an order by the Privy Council,
to the Bishops of all the dioceses, to see that it was
read and taught in all grammar schools.

One requirement of some schools—in connexion
with physical exercises—may be mentioned, *e.g.* in
the Orders of Harrow School: ' You shall allow
your child at all times, bow-shafts, bow-strings and a

bracer, to exercise *shooting* [*i.e.* archery].' At Eton 'the Shooting Fields' probably denoted the provision for the pursuit of the same exercise. Archery is referred to in the School Statutes of St Albans, 1578, and of Dedham School, 1579. Whatever criticisms we pass on the old grammar schools, they helped to train the men who repelled the Spanish Armada, and to build up the heroes on both sides in the great Civil War.


CHAPTER X

THE DECADENCE OF GRAMMAR SCHOOLS AND THE
RISE OF THE 'GREAT PUBLIC SCHOOLS.'

We can judge of the vitality of the grammar school as an institution from the eagerness for its plantation in the New England colonies by the English emigrants who had experienced at home the value of a classical training, for it was a common maxim of the 17th century in England : ' better unborn than untaught.' The question naturally arises : How is it that, in the 20th century, there is so much adverse criticism and even contempt for the idea of classical studies, amongst the great mass of the people, among successful merchants and manufacturers, as well as among tradesmen and farmers. The

17th century parent was not in better worldly cir-
cumstances.  The New England colonist had enough
to do, without troubling about 'learning,' in working his way in a new country, often with Indians
to subdue or to conciliate, as well as in exerting
efforts incident to tilling the soil, or in the work of
other industries.  On *a priori* grounds, the colonist
was the most unlikely of men to cry out for grammar
schools, and the founding of grammar schools the
most unlikely of directions in which the richer men
could be expected to spend their spare money, or
for which to bequeath their possessions.

One reason for the modern change of attitude
is clear.  The enormous rush and hurry of modern
life have made all enterprises requiring time and
waiting relatively undesirable, or at least unde-
sired, however important their final value.  'We
have not time for culture,' it is said.  'Culture is
aesthetic in nature, and must be relegated to the
leisure moments of life,' which is almost like suggesting to defer the matter till the Greek Kalends.
For the state of leisure—that attitude of mind which
gave the idea of 'school' to the Greeks is alien to
the active life of to-day, just as to the mind of Burke
in contemplating the French Revolution 'the age of
chivalry *is gone* ! '

But the grammar school stood to the New
England colonist, as it had stood to Renascence

England, for the spirit of humanism ; and modern
life can no more afford to lose that spirit than could
any age in the past. The essence of humanism is
democratic, as much a message to the artisan
and the peasant as to the scholar. We have seen
that it meant a great deal to yeomen, grocers,
drapers, skinners, etc., in the past, who were willing
to give up their means to support it—as far as they
could—worthily. The value of ' higher' studies was
understood in the 16th and 17th centuries, though
often expressed in terms that somewhat too narrowly
confined humanism to Christian doctrine on the one
hand, or to stylistic classicism on the other. If we
can interpret him in the truly humanistic sense,
Erasmus may be the spokesman of what the grammar
schools came to stand for, in spite of all their variety
and all their narrowness. ' The sun itself is not more
common and open to all than the teaching of Christ. . .
I wish that even the weakest woman should read
the Gospel—should read the Epistles of Paul. . . *To
make them understood is surely the first step.* It may
be that they might be ridiculed by many, but some
would take them to heart. I long that the husband-
man should sing portions of them to himself as he
follows the plough, that the weaver should hum them
to the tune of his shuttle, that the traveller should
beguile with their stories the tedium of his journey.'
Does it seem futile to look for this spirit of

'understanding' in the present age, when we contemplate the changed conditions of the modern world of factories, warehouses, and the rows of benches of clerks? If so, let us reflect on the fact that these words of Erasmus were, in some ways, an underestimate of prophecy of what actually was largely realised under the educational training of the old grammar schools. For all classes of the community were accepted, often the *poorest* had the preference. Education was cheap; there were numerous grants and often the personal interest and supervision of the learned in the neighbourhood. To all, the key to the highest culture of the age was offered. The object of the grammar school, from the point of view of humanism, is to give the mental training which can best serve to help to lead each individual to realise for himself the best and noblest that has been done in history, and written in literature. To the 16th and 17th centuries the subject-matter was mainly concerned with Palestine, Rome and Greece, with the Bible, Cicero and Homer. The spirit of the grammar school does not necessarily involve the retention of these old-world studies, but if it could speak, it would seriously inquire how far the proposed substitutes would at least attempt to stimulate the same earnest attitude to life which the old grammar school endeavoured to induce, namely, in the eloquent words of Milton, ' to lead and draw pupils in willing obedience, inflamed with the study of learning, and the admiration of virtue; stirred up with high hopes of living to be brave men, and worthy patriots, dear to God, and famous to all ages.'

There is no doubt as to the decadence of the grammar schools from 1660 onwards. No less a man than the philosopher Thomas Hobbes paid the old grammar schools the compliment of protesting against them, on the ground that the boys became so impressed by the studies of the civil conflicts which had taken place in the pursuit of liberty in ancient Greece and Rome, that when they became men they sought to emulate the ancients by a civil war against their king. As an advocate of absolute power in the monarch he boldly declared against classics being taught, for that reason. The growth and development of a vernacular literature naturally introduced the conflicting claims of the study of national as against Latin literature, and Locke showed how important the foreign learned works, especially French, had become, so that in many branches of knowledge it was clear, in a way that it was not clear, say to Milton, in the preceding generation, that modern text-books were better adapted to modern needs than the treatises of ancient classical writers on the same subjects. Defoe pointed out that not one sea-faring man in twenty understood Latin, yet a man could be a good navigator

without it.  Going further than Locke, Defoe boldly
affirmed (showing that the classical tradition for him
was broken down in its last corner of defence), ' you
can be a gentleman of learning, and yet reading in
English may do all for you that you want.' In other
words, utilitarianism had become the watchword
of a new age, and to meet this want other kinds of
schools were instituted, following examples in France
and in Germany; and stimulated by the needs of the
increased population of the country, attention began,
after the Restoration, to be concentrated on the
elementary education, on that reading and writing,
which the grammar schools had so determinedly
refused to admit as part of their work.  Thus the
educational effort of the philanthropic and personal
kind which, in pre-Restoration times had been
lavished on the grammar schools, was now transferred to the charity schools, and since these were
established mainly by the Church of England, they
became ' feeders ' for passing on the children into
membership of the Church after the school-age.  The
dissenters in the 18th century, however, in the first instance took an active part in the foundation of charity
schools, and in the 18th century they provided about
one-tenth or one-twelfth of the total number, as
Mr de Montmorency says.  The Society for Promoting
Christian Knowledge, which organised these charity
schools for the Church of England, was founded in

1698, and by 1729 had helped to establish over 1600 schools with 34,000 children. Addison describes the charity schools as 'the glory of the age.' In the latter part of the 18th century, the popular interest was centred in the development of Sunday schools.

It was felt, consciously or unconsciously, by the attached Royalists that Hobbes was not altogether wrong in thinking that the grammar schools had helped to produce the doughty champions of the Parliamentarians, men like Selden (Chichester Grammar School), John Hampden (Thame Grammar School), John Milton (St Paul's), and the redoubtable Oliver Cromwell himself (Huntingdon Grammar School). They argued about legal precedents, and appealed to documents of old English rights and liberties with an antiquarian zeal and readiness, evidently due to the scholarly methods of inquiry of which the grammar schools had sown the seeds. For they had provided the atmosphere for at any rate the foundations of severe classical studies, which pupils afterwards further developed in the universities. The later Stuart kings and their advisers accordingly felt no desire to go out of their way in the encouragement of the old schools. Charles II, in as far as he showed interest in schools, did so by imitation of French models, and turned his royal attention to the foundation of the Mathematical School as a separate department in Christ's Hospital. In the 18th

century, ' English ' schools began to flourish, founded
sometimes in conjunction with grammar or 'Latin'
schools, and sometimes independently of them. But,
further, one of the features of the 18th century, educationally, at the secondary grade, was the rise of the
private schools, the direct outcome of the expansion
of the old 'writing' and 'arithmetic' schools. These
schools sometimes provided Latin, mathematics,
and French, or one or other of them. If they taught
Latin, they were called 'private Grammar Schools.'
Another set of private schools developed from the
schools for the teaching of modern languages, particularly French and Italian. Pupils of grammar
schools and others had frequented these schools as
supplementary to classical education, but in the
latter part of the 17th, and in the 18th, century, schools kept by foreigners which began as
modern language schools added also the teaching
of Latin and arithmetic and other subjects, and
thus became substantially private grammar schools.
It was held even in 1805 that an endowed ' Grammar
School ' could not, legally, be allowed to introduce
other subjects—modern languages, or even mathematics—and this decision was only overruled by an
Act of Parliament in 1840. In the 18th century, therefore, the grammar schools, with statutes limiting the
curriculum to the teaching of the Latin and Greek
languages, and to religious instruction, could not

withstand the competition of the other types of school, which developed with unexampled rapidity. Most of the private grammar schools supplied exactly what was wanted, *i.e.* they were ' practical ' and ' commercial.' Others continued the old classical tradition, although ' illegally ' including further subjects. Teaching became a good business when well managed, and the old advertisements in the newly rising periodicals show in many cases the flashy pretensions, whilst the wages paid to the drudges of ushers reveal unconsciously the shallowness of the new type of school.    Still, the bishops refrained from interfering with these private venture schools, reserving their vigilance for dealing with the Nonconformists on account of their refusal to conform, rather than interesting themselves in any proved pedagogic disqualifications.    The consequence was that the Nonconformist schools and academies learned that the only way even to go on existing, was to have a full belief in the task of education, and to maintain the highest aims of scholarship, so as to produce that type of mind in their pupils which would be able to hold its own on a high level in controversy and in the practice of life.    Their schools and academies, accordingly, were probably the soundest educational establishments of the 18th century, and as they could not easily become settled institutions, each individual school had to think

out for itself afresh its methods and even its curriculum. Yet the classics, though in a modified form,
were taught both intensively and extensively, sufficiently to entitle the *Academies* to rank essentially
as grammar schools and as classical colleges.

Owing to the competing forces of avowedly
elementary schools, of the charity schools, of private
grammar and commercial schools, of the dissenting grammar schools and academies, the clientèle
from which the old endowed grammar schools
could draw became more and more limited. The
wide-awake, practical parents sent their children
to schools which laid claim (whether adequately
or inadequately, rightly or wrongly, they had not
time or judgment to inquire) to move with the times.
The dissenters, of conscientious convictions, wished
their children to be taught by their own ministers, or at
least by those teachers who were not out of sympathy
with their point of view. Many held that an elementary education was sufficient and the sooner the
child went to apprenticeship the better. When the
nation was united in religion, the grammar school on
the whole had attracted the best of the 'wits' amongst
the boys. In the 18th century the grammar schools
got only the leavings. Many parents for one reason
or another preferred to send children to the private
schools where they paid fees, rather than to the old
grammar schools, even when they were free.

No doubt the loosening of the bonds of the old puritanic rigour of religion and life, at the Restoration, was partly the cause. The rebound to the secular side of life naturally told against the ' schools of learning ' since learning had actually been allied with religion of the puritan type, as closely as Hobbes thought it had been associated with politics. And so another small but important class of the community preferred to send their children away from all the English schools with their growingly conflicting interests, and settled them either in foreign schools, or more frequently with learned Huguenot pastors or foreign scholars. Similarly Leyden often proved a resort for English students at the university stage.

But at the back of all these contributory causes, there was the further ground of the decadence in standing, in qualifications, in directness of teaching aims, and in religious force of character, of the average grammar schoolmaster of the 18th century. In 1795, Lord Chief Justice Kenyon spoke of the lamentable state of the grammar schools, ' *empty walls without scholars, and everything neglected* but the receipt of the salaries and emoluments.' The 18th century, however, had its extraordinary grammar scholars, and schoolmasters; and if we are obliged to regard the school-territory of the period as a low-lying, unpleasant plain, on the whole, there were in it peaks which rose up in lonely splendour, more outstanding perhaps than in any other age of English history.  We have to acknowledge the splendid 18th century scholar Richard Bentley, Master of Trinity College, Cambridge, 1700–42, whom Henry Hallam described in his survey of the history of European Literature, as ' the greatest of English [classical] critics in this, or possibly any other age,' a judgment which is not likely to be gainsaid.  Bentley was connected with grammar school history, in a two-fold bond ; he was educated at Wakefield Grammar School, and for a year Spalding Grammar School was honoured by his presence as headmaster. Richard Porson was a classical scholar of enormous power of memory and of unusual Greek erudition. He was educated at Eton, though he went there somewhat late.  Samuel Parr was a third remarkable scholar.  In his sixth year he entered Harrow ; at 14 years of age he was head boy of the school. After 14 months at Cambridge he returned to Harrow School as first assistant, and when the headmaster died in 1771 was an applicant for the post.  In pique at his non-appointment he started a rival school at Stanmore, to which he drew off 40 Harrovian boys, but owing to his strange, if not irresponsible conduct, the school was a failure.  He then became headmaster of Colchester Grammar School in 1777, and in the next year passed on as headmaster to

Norwich Grammar School, which he left in 1785. He next opened a private academy at Hatton, near Warwick. To mediocre boys he was indulgent but he was a determined flogger of ' the really talented.' Parr wrote in distinctive Ciceronian style in Latin, and in exaggerated Johnsonese in English. But the figure that specially fills the 18th century stage of literature is not the greatest of the classical scholars, Bentley, or the strange and less learned scholars, Porson and Parr, but Samuel Johnson, who had been a pupil at Lichfield Grammar School and afterwards at Stourbridge Grammar School where he helped to teach the younger boys. He also taught as an usher at Market Bosworth Grammar School. Moreover Johnson was an unsuccessful candidate for the mastership of Appleby Grammar School, declaring ' that it would make him happy for life ' if he were appointed.

But such examples, though they may be considered to more than justify the renown of individual schools, cannot be multiplied so as to remove the grammar schools of the 18th century from the adverse judgment of Lord Kenyon, mentioned above. Two of the 18th century schoolmasters call for mention, for if a couple of whole-hearted schoolmasters could have saved the rest, it would have been done by the two different types of men, Vicesimus Knox and Thomas James, the former the headmaster of Ton-

bridge Grammar School ; the latter, the distinguished
and successful headmaster of Rugby in the 18th
century.

For Knox, Samuel Johnson as well as the Oxford
academic authorities prophesied a brilliant scholarly career, and dissuaded him from entering upon
schoolmastering, a profession which they feared
' would engross him.' So it proved, and in his
*Liberal Education*, in 1781, Knox wrote an en-
thusiastic volume on the practical side of grammar
school education. Whilst he attempted to encourage
fellow grammar schoolmasters by the inspiration of
his belief in classical aims, and afforded assistance by
his suggestions of classical resources and methods,
he combated the shallow pretentiousness of the
new private adventure schools, whose proprietors
sheltered themselves behind the speculative opinions
of educational thinkers like Locke. Knox pointed
out that new directions of curricula, in mathematics,
modern languages, and natural sciences, depend
for their educational value upon efficient methods
of teaching—in which Knox was, no doubt, right
in believing there had not been sufficient tested
development to place them beside the pedagogic
discipline of the classics, the teaching of which had
been the growth of centuries of educational experience and thought.

It was in the 18th century, too, despite the

general decadence, that the old grammar schools of
Eton, Winchester, Westminster, Harrow and Rugby
won their distinctive position, from which they
developed into a group and together with St Paul's,
Merchant Taylors', Charterhouse, and Shrewsbury,
constitute the 'Public Schools' of the Royal Commission of 1864.    Some other schools may now
justifiably be termed 'great' and 'Public.'    But all
old endowed schools, 'Public' or otherwise, were,
originally, grammar schools.    It was within the
18th century that Edward Barnard, 'the Pitt of
masters,' ruled at Eton ; a worthy forerunner of
the Arnold spirit at Rugby.    Winchester had its
Joseph Warton.    Westminster can rejoice in having
had its John Nicoll, probably 'not a whit behind'
the illustrious Richard Busby of the 17th century,
as a headmaster.    It was in the 18th century,
too, that Harrow rose to marked success under
Dr Thomas Thackeray.    Rugby prospered to such an
extent under Thomas James that, though the number
in the school was only 52 when he came in 1778,
the register stood at 245 boys in the school when he
left in 1794.    Nor is it necessary to more than recall
the fact that Thomas Arnold reinforced by further
developments James's manly and noble methods
of control, by introducing a larger share of assistance
in self-government and in the influence of the senior
boys at Rugby.    Nor must it be left unmentioned,

that the mantle of Dr James fell upon his ' old boy,'
Samuel Butler, when he took up the headmastership of Shrewsbury School in 1798. But all
these men, amongst the greatest in the whole history
of schoolmasters, had to contend with arrears of
slackness, and of rebellion against their predecessors
in this same 18th century, and only pulled through
to success by the greatest determination. The
general state of the schools was deplorable.

The 19th century saw its Arnold of Rugby and
its Thring of Uppingham, who directly influenced
and drew upwards the standard of tone and work,
not only in the great ' Public ' Schools, but also in
a small, better section of the old grammar schools.
The Endowed Schools Inquiry Commission of 1864–8
made the most searching inquiry into the old schools.
Sir Joshua Fitch has summarised the experience of
the Commissioners as to the state of the schools :
' The number of scholars who were obtaining the
sort of education in Latin and Greek contemplated
by the founders was very small, and was constantly
diminishing ; the general instruction in other subjects was found to be very worthless, the very
existence of statutes prescribing the ancient learning
often serving as a reason for the absence of all teaching of modern subjects ; and, with a few honourable
exceptions, the endowed schools were found to be
characterised by inefficient supervision on the part

of the governing bodies and by languor and feeble-
ness on the part of teachers and taught.' 'I know,'
adds Fitch, ' no more melancholy chapter in English
history than is supplied by the ponderous volumes
of the Schools Inquiry Commission.  It is a history
of great resources wasted, of high hopes frustrated
and of means and plans wholly unsuited to the ends
proposed to be attained.'

The closing decades of the 19th century and the
early years of the 20th promise a very different
future opening out before these schools.  Two great
legislative measures following upon the report of
the Commission of Inquiry have led to this great
change.  The Public Schools Act of 1868 dealt with
the great Public Schools of Winchester, Eton,
Shrewsbury, Westminster, Rugby, Harrow, Charterhouse, St Paul's and Merchant Taylors', providing
for the appointment of new governors, who were to
draw up revised statutes and regulations, subject to
the approval of the Privy Council.  The next year,
1869, the much larger body of endowed Secondary
Schools came under the drastic operation of the
Endowed Schools Act which referred the drawing up
of new schemes for their administration, in the first
place, to Special Commissioners.  Afterwards, in
1874, the power of control was transferred to the
Charity Commissioners, and in 1899 was vested in
the Board of Education.  The Endowed Schools Act

broadened the outlook. For instance, it was laid down that, as far as possible, provision was to be made 'for extending to girls the benefits of the educational endowments.' New confidence was thus inspired in the future possibilities of the old grammar schools. Within the schools there was a widening of curriculum, by the inclusion of modern subjects, particularly foreign languages and sciences ; and mathematics were made a part of every grammar school scheme.

The Education Act of 1902 has led to the establishment, alongside of the old endowed grammar schools, of a still larger number of new municipal and county secondary schools of a more restrictedly 'modern' commercial, and industrial type. The result has been on the one hand, to stimulate old grammar schools into more practical alertness, whilst, on the other hand, the grammar school draws the municipal schools towards a closer effort to supply a 'liberal education.'

The value of the grammar school—in the sense of the classical school—to the community has by no means been superseded. We have seen it has noble traditions behind it ; and it proceeds along the line of historical continuity, though, of course, it must adapt itself to modern conditions of scholarship and, we may add, of pedagogical methods. Its great necessity is to insist on quality of work and

well-selected pupils rather than on numbers in the
school register. It continues to stand for an element in
the national life, proved by centuries of experience to
be of the first importance, viz. the training in humanism, the point of contact between past, present and
future, in thought and its expression, brought to
bear on the permanent in life. It represents, in our
educational organisation, the element which recog-
nises that 'there has never been a time when much
of the best training of the mind did not consist in
the study of the thought of the past recorded in
a language, not the student's own[1].' The democrati-
sation of education has laid special emphasis on
the necessity of the addition of the limitation '*for
chosen pupils only*,' but the principle of the old
grammar schools is as necessary as ever nationally,
in its due perspective.

[1] A. S. Wilkins, *Roman Education*, p. 20.

# SHORT BIBLIOGRAPHY

ACKERMANN, R. *History of the Colleges of Winchester, Eton and Westminster, the Charterhouse, the Schools of St Paul's, Merchant Taylors', Harrow, Rugby, and Christ's Hospital.* London, 1816.

BARNARD, HENRY. *English Pedagogy.* Series I and II. Hartford, U.S.A., 1876.

BRINSLEY, JOHN. *Ludus Literarius, or the Grammar School.* London, 1612.

BROWN, ELMER E. *The Making of our Middle Schools.* New York, 1907.

CARLISLE, NICHOLAS. *A Concise Description of the Endowed Grammar Schools in England and Wales.* 2 vols. London, 1818.

CHANDLER, R. *The Life of William Waynflete.* London, 1811.

CHURTON, RALPH. *The life of Alexander Nowell.* Oxford, 1809.

COLE, Sir HENRY. *King Henry VIII's Scheme of Bishopricks ...with some notices of the State of Popular Education.* London, 1838.

DE MONTMORENCY, J. E. G. *State Intervention in English Education.* Cambridge, 1902.

HAZLITT, W. C. *Schools, School books, and Schoolmasters.* London, 1888.

HOOLE, CHARLES. *A New Discoverie of the Old Art of Keeping Schools.* London, 1660. Edited with Bibliographical Index by E. T. Campagnac. London: Constable, 1913.

LEACH, A. F. *Educational Charters and Documents*, 598 *to* 1909 A.D. Cambridge, 1911. *English Schools at the Reformation*, 1546–8. London, 1896. *Early Yorkshire Schools*, Vol. I. York, Beverley, Ripon. Vol. II. Pontefract, Howden, Northallerton, Acaster, Rotherham, Giggleswick, Sedbergh. Yorkshire Archaeological Society. Record Series, Vols. XXVII and XXXIII.

LUPTON, J. H. *A Life of Dean Colet*. London, 1887.

LYTE, Sir H. C. MAXWELL. *A History of Eton College*. 4th edition. London, 1911.

MULLINGER, J. BASS. *The Schools of Charles the Great and the Restoration of Education in the Ninth Century*. London, 1877.

Schools Inquiry Commission. 12 volumes. 1869.

STAUNTON, HOWARD. *The Great Schools of England*. London, 1869.

STOWE, A. MONROE. *English Grammar Schools in the reign of Queen Elizabeth*. Columbia University, New York, 1908.

TIMBS, JOHN. *School-days of Eminent Men*. London, 1858.

WALCOTT, M. E. C. *William of Wykeham and his Colleges*. Winchester and London, 1852.

WASE, CHRISTOPHER. *Considerations concerning Free Schools as settled in England*. Oxford, 1678.

WHISTON, ROBERT. *Cathedral Trusts and their Fulfilment*. London, 1849.

WEST, A. F. *Alcuin and the Rise of the Christian Schools*. Great Educators Series. London, 1893.

WILKINS, A. S. *National Education in Greece*. London, 1873. *Roman Education*. Cambridge, 1905.

## ACCOUNTS OF SEPARATE SCHOOLS.

A. F. LEACH. *Articles on Schools in the Victoria County Histories,* in progress. *A History of Winchester College.* London, 1899. See also above, p. 144.

Most of the historical accounts of old grammar schools are either in local histories of the towns, or in School Magazines, though there is happily a tendency to publish monographs of those of which the history can still be traced. The most comprehensive history of an English school is that of Eton by Sir H. C. Maxwell Lyte (see above, p. 144) though that of Merchant Taylors' School by the Rev. H. B. Wilson in 1814, is a record of exact and full detail up to that date. Messrs Methuen have published a Series of School 'Annals,' including Eton, Westminster, Shrewsbury, Christ's Hospital. Messrs Duckworth also issued a Public School Series including Winchester, Eton, Rugby. Unfortunately, neither of these Series was completed by the inclusion of all the Public Schools.

Further lists of works on a considerable number of separate schools are given in:

(1) A. M. Stowe: *English Grammar Schools in the reign of Queen Elizabeth,* pp. 196–200.

(2) W. S. SONNENSCHEIN: *Best Books* (1912 edition), Part II, pp. 735–739.

# INDEX

## DATE DUE

| | | | |
|---|---|---|---|
| | | | |
| | | | |
| | | | |
| | | | |
| | | | |
| | | | |
| | | | |
| | | | |
| | | | |
| | | | |
| | | | |
| | | | |
| | | | |
| | | | |
| | | | |
| | | | |
| | | | |
| | | | |
| | | | |